The *Forgotten Arts*

YESTERDAY'S TECHNIQUES ADAPTED TO TODAY'S MATERIALS

by Richard M. Bacon

BOOK ONE

Published MCMLXXV by
YANKEE, INC.
Dublin, New Hampshire
03444

This Book Has Been Prepared by the Staff of Yankee, Inc.

Clarissa M. Silitch, Editor
Carl F. Kirkpatrick, Art Director

First Edition
Copyright 1975, by Yankee, Inc.
Printed in the United States of America

Seventh Printing 1981

Library of Congress Catalog Card No. 75-10770
ISBN-0-911658-65-3

Contents

Foreword

The Art of Country Living

For everything there is a season. The man living on the land today must learn to accept forces that dictate his life as they did those of his rural forebears, to adapt his ways to the cycles of the seasons, to plan his time — days, weeks, and even years ahead — and to enjoy each bounty as it is offered in his quest for a life of self-reliance.

Even in New England it is still possible and practical to raise a good portion of one's food in a little space and a short season. The land also provides fuel for cooking and heating, material for houses and barns, and a variety of products that will sustain both body and mind.

Despite the most careful and imaginative planning, there will still be too little time to accomplish everything. There will be projects that fail, harvests that do not live up to expectations, surpluses that spoil because they come too quickly and too soon, and animals that do not thrive. Learning to live with setbacks is a real part of rural life.

Monotony lurks in every corner for those who wear blinders. There are chores that cannot be postponed: wood to cut and carry, animals to tend, snow to move, seeds to plant and crops to harvest, meals to prepare. Life dominated by the weather and limited by the physical horizon can doom the countryman to mere subsistence, to lifeless resignation. Or it can be used to firm his convictions of what it is to be alive. For those who live with the seasons, demands not only come in cycles but in waves that are often interwoven. One thing leads to another. An unused item challenges one to find a use for it. There is endless opportunity for rediscovery — finding different ways of using what you grow, growing what you need, and eliminating inessentials from life.

Moreover, within routine there is a chance for wonder — a chance to expand one's inner resources as each familiar season reappears. In this striving for a balanced life there must be time to stand and stare — to know the quiet friendliness of a well-stocked barn; to amble up the hill pasture just to speculate; to swim in the pond after the heat and dust of haying; to sit relaxed with friends and talk; to dream up ways of making entertainment personal again — these are also rightful harvests for the countryman today.

To live in a rural setting does not mean the rejection of everything modern. Four-wheel drive, national public radio, and hot showers all allow a lifestyle and freedom that was not dreamt of by our grandparents whose roots sprang from the very land that nurtures us.

For every practitioner of the arts of country living, there are thousands who are doing the same things in slightly different ways. Each is pursuing his personal quest for meaning, enjoyment, and fulfillment.

R. M. B.

Managing the Small Woodlot

O NCE THE HOME WOODLOT STOOD like money in the bank. It was drawn upon for seasonal needs and sometimes depleted in times of emergency. Woodlot operation was an integral part of a system of inter-related activities on the New England family farm. Wood was taken from it to heat the home and cook meals; poles and posts fenced the pastures; lumber was there for beams, planks, boards and shingles, for home repair and new construc-tion; sawlogs were sold to local mills for cash profit. Enough timber was left growing—hopefully—to allow the farmer's widow and children, if need arose, to carry on.

Today, as many professional for-esters agree, the small woodlot own-er, with holdings of from 10 to 50 acres, is doing less and less in his woods each year. This lack of activ-ity and interest is due to a change in life style and a shift in personal pri-orities. Most heads of households earn their living away from home. With their salaries they can buy fuel and building supplies. For recre-ation many find it more exciting to snowmobile through the winter woods than to work in them.

It is also partly due to an environ-mental concern in which the in-junction to "spare that tree"—voiced in the 1830s and intended to slow down the greedy lumber bar-ons—is being taken literally.

A new generation of landowners has arrived, and many of them don't realize the possibilities their wood-lots offer. They also don't know how to begin—or where.*

---

*NOTE: Before doing anything on property you think is yours, you should find out exact-ly *where* your boundaries are. We know of at least two cases where people have managed their neighbor's woodlot for a number of years before anybody discovered the mistake.

What are some of the assets of a properly managed woodlot? The most obvious, perhaps, are lumber and cordwood. But there are by-products worth considering: sap for maple syrup and sugar; edible wild plants, fruits, and nuts; material for landscaping; provision of windbreaks, Christmas trees, and privacy; areas for camping and wildlife sanctuaries; trails for hiking, horseback riding, cross-country skiing, learning—or just plain loafing.

Ben Rice—the man who for a quarter of a century has written the country essays facing the calendar pages in *The Old Farmer's Almanac* —has given a lot of thought and energy to his family woodlot and has also voiced concern about the future use of forests in general. He and his wife own property which has been in the family since 1896. Their ownership, he says, is not without restrictions and considerations and judgments not necessarily their own.

Since 1938, when the Rices bought the land from his father, they have been carrying on good silviculture practices on the advice of their county forester. Roads have been kept open for accessibility and fire protection. Ponds have been created in cooperation with the Soil Conservation Service. The owners have set out seedling plantations of red pine bought from the state nursery. They have thinned and weeded and sometimes pruned the natural forest. On several occasions, under the management of an experienced forester, the Rices have cut and sold under contract selectively marked timber on the stump. And the woods, in time,

have profited from this care.

But bringing a woodlot into prime condition is a long and slow business. Proper woodlot management, according to Henry I. Baldwin, retired research forester for the State of New Hampshire, is like tending a summer garden. It takes periodic cultivation and a plan of attack to achieve the best results.

Contrary to a centuries-old European tradition, Americans have followed a policy of taking the best trees and leaving the worst. This approach has left most of New England—a natural forest area—covered by a poor quality of second- and third-growth timber.

Wood is one of our few renewable resources. As a fuel—and unlike coal, gas and oil—it reproduces itself. If only for its value as a fuel, then, the family woodlot can continually supply the homestead with enough cordage to withstand the cold New England winters. Even if not used as the primary heat source, fireplace and stove wood can be used greatly to reduce the need for other fuels. Hickory, white oak and beech will give out the most heat. Sugar maple, red oak and birch are also dependable. Red maple is less desirable while pine and aspen are both low energy producers. Green wood will burn but the heat it gives is low, and, because it may spark, the danger of chimney fires is increased.

A common measurement for firewood is the cord—a stack 8 feet long, 4 feet high, and 4 feet deep. Large logs should be split as soon as possible to hasten the drying process. Trees intended for the woodshed are often felled while the foliage is still green. Woodsmen then leave the trees where they are for several weeks; the leaves will help draw out the moisture content from the trunk. Later they return, limb the tree, and cut it into 4-foot lengths. Many leave the cords of cut lengths in the woods to air dry for several months (fuel wood should be dried 4 to 12 months or more before it is used), then skid them to the woodshed after the ground is frozen.

For this operation you will need a saw and an ax. Chain saws are common even among small woodlot owners, but a two-man saw and a buck saw also come in handy. For splitting wood you should have a maul, a pair of metal wedges, and a sledge hammer. All tools should be sharp and in good working order.

January is the month to prune and trim, to weed and thin your woodlot, and to yard the wood to the roadside before accumulated snows of deep winter make access more difficult. It is also the time to skid sawlogs out of the woods and pile them

conveniently so they can be trucked to the mill. But most small woodlot owners today do not have the time, the knowledge, or the equipment to harvest sawlogs. Cuttings are usually contracted to local lumbermen with the advice of the county forester. When trees to harvest have been marked, selective or clear cutting decided upon, an agreement for harvest and payment is struck.

The demand for many woodlot products has diminished. Mr. Baldwin cites the falling market for wooden boxes, turnery, excelsior, veneer in small lots, tanbark and charcoal.

Sawlogs are still competed for, and in this fuel crisis so is cordwood for fireplaces and stoves. However, to the urban dweller, this is still a luxury item. According to Bob Breck, Hillsboro (N.H.) County Forester who has been covering the same territory for the last 25 years, stumpage rates (standing timber) have recently risen considerably. There is also apparently no end in sight for the consumption of wood pulp

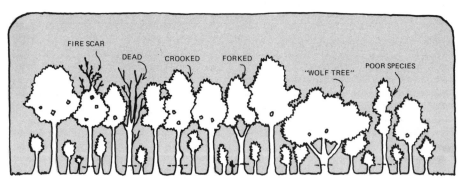

Before improvement cutting

in the manufacture of paper products.

The small woodlot can supply top-quality sawlogs if properly managed over a long period of time. But it will take more years than most people have. A marketable white pine—20 inches in diameter at breast height—must grow for about 80 years. According to records Breck has been keeping, the average diameter growth of white pine—considered a desirable and fast-growing species —is less than two-tenths of an inch a year even in a managed woodlot.

"Most people don't even think about tomorrow," Bob Breck says. "A prime hardwood will take another 20 to 40 years to grow, and when you start talking in terms of four generations to a lot of them, you might as well be talking about eternity."

He realizes an interest in managing forests for higher production has been replaced by a concern for preservation in the natural state—for trails, ponds, recreation and sports. "Because of taxes," he says, "mere preservation is a luxury few people can really afford." Breck believes in conservation, the keystone of which is use, but not abuse.

Pruning is often practiced to produce a white pine log that is clean and knot-free. (Another 30 years is added before harvest if enough new wood is to develop over the knot.) To prune—and often it is necessary if only to open up vistas, reduce the danger of fire or the invasion of insects, or to cut back trails and roads —use a pruning saw, never an ax. The saw can be attached to a pole up to 12 feet long and will make a neat cut close to the tree trunk. The ax may leave a jagged limb butt and scar the bark, thereby permitting easier entrance of disease organisms. Shrubs can be pruned with long-handled pruning shears. Experiments have been made using a club to prune both living and dead branches at various temperatures. But the results are inconclusive and seem to depend on the variety of tree.

Wood cut for poles and posts should be peeled to prevent insect

After improvement cutting

damage beneath the bark while it is drying. This is most easily done when the wood is still in the green stage. Red pine poles should be harvested in May, not in the fall. This will prevent staining and rotting. In addition, in late spring they will dry out more quickly, be light to handle, and remain durable.

Thinning, weeding and liberation cutting in your woodlot are more necessary than pruning and have the advantage of allowing you to see the results and use the wood more quickly. These operations release prime trees to grow from 15 feet to 20 feet apart, increase the amount of sunlight, reduce the chance of insects and diseases, and release more moisture and soil nutrients. Thinning out unwanted trees—weed trees and those deformed, diseased and rotting—is not only good silviculture, but also will provide pulpwood and fuel, fence posts, and poles for the garden.

"Some woodlot owners," Breck says, "fight to save specific trees which are of no worth. They might be deformed and look like giant cabbages, or have heart rot or cankers. These should be felled to allow something better to grow in their place."

What should you, the woodlot owner, do first? Get in touch with your county forester and arrange to meet him on the lot. Go around with him and observe. Discuss the vari-ous possibilities your land suggests for developing wood products as well as some of the by-products humans and wild life crave. Then cooperate in making a workable and realistic plan.

"Just keep pecking away," Breck concludes. "If a small woodlot owner would spend even a day a month in some kind of consistent weeding and thinning program, in 25 years he would have made a prime start."

But there is another value the woodlot owner can set upon his land —not because he owns it, for in the true sense of ownership he is merely its custodian for a brief period in the life of the forest. As Ben Rice says, "When I walk through these old groves, I find what I can find nowhere else in this troubled world— a sense of peace, of timelessness. The only clocks in the forest are the four seasons. Here, each moment is eternity."

References
The best reference for woodlot management is your county forester. He will not only give you advice on how to proceed but will supply you with information and material for study. You can also secure government pamphlets on forestry from your county agent and state university.

Cooking on a Wood Stove

WOOD COOKSTOVES OFTEN HAVE more individual quirks than the cooks who use them. But successful cooking with wood begins in the woodshed. The key to a well-planned and tasty meal is the availability and selection of fuel—split, dried and stacked perhaps a year in advance.

There are innumerable advantages to cooking with one's own wood. A 20-acre woodlot will supply a family's cooking and heating needs almost indefinitely, if culled and harvested properly. The cost of wood grown on the farm is lower than that of any other fuel. In addition, wood cookstoves continue to function when outside power sources fail. They provide auxiliary heat, and this in turn can make a kitchen the family social center that modern efficiency has done its best to displace.

It is true that bread can be baked in any oven, but somehow the combined odors of fresh bread and a wood stove are enough to stir a pang of nostalgia in any breast.

However, before installing a wood cookstove in your kitchen—if you are fortunate enough to locate one in working order at a reasonable price—consider some of the *dis*advantages. Foremost is the amount of wood demanded by the cook to keep meals coming on time. If it is available and at hand, wood-stove cooking is economical. But the constant cutting, dragging, splitting, stacking, and carting of wood into the kitchen can be a tiresome task in a busy world and has persuaded many a farm boy to leave for the city.

11

Cooking with wood is dirty. Not only are wood ashes shifty things with wills of their own, but pots and skillets—especially if fitted into the lid holes for faster, hotter results —are miserable to clean and cannot be set on a countertop without leaving sooty rings.

Any wood fire in the home is a potential fire hazard; therefore, the chimney must be in perfect order and both it and the stove must be periodically checked and cleaned.

Finally—although a plate of biscuits in a wood-stove oven is still only 15 minutes away from the table when the men come in from 'coon hunting at 2:00 A.M.—cooking on a wood stove is not as quick, easy, and convenient as the modern gas or electric range. The wood stove has no place in a household where the cook has another job unless it is either a second stove or merely a conversation piece. It takes a lot of damper-jiggling, stoking, and persistence to achieve satisfying results.

In learning the art of wood-stove cooking—even if one is already a capable cook using another fuel— there are bound to be disappointments until the personalities of cook and stove become compatible.

To start with, the fuel must be dry. Although any wood will burn eventually, the fire will be hotter and more easily controlled if seasoned wood is used. Green wood can provoke chimney fires.

Hereabouts, the stove wood most generally used is white or rock maple, beech, white birch, and white or red oak. Ash is a fine wood, easily split and safe to use either green or dry. In the old days ash was used largely as kindling. It was split into 3/4-inch vertical slabs, then these were worked into 3/4-inch square sticks with a hatchet. Small-diameter ash was left in the round.

Countrymen never use pine, even for kindling. This wood can coat your chimney with resin, which in turn could lead to a house burning. Pine is saved for the lumber yard.

Wood that will not split easily because of knots or grain is stacked in another area of the woodshed and eventually finds its way to the parlor stove.

In the days when the wood range was king of the kitchen, country people kept a woodbox next to it, which was filled with a mixed lot of stove-length wood by the boys before they went to bed. From this the cook would select her fuel for the purpose intended: birch for a quick, hot fire with little body; maple and beech for longer-lasting dependability; oak (which takes longer to dry) for a slow, hot fire, once a bed of coals had been established. It was an unsplit oak log that was put into the firebox just before bedtime and banked with ashes. Usually the cookstove firebox was too small to hold a fire to last the night (a larger one would make it more difficult to adjust cooking temperatures), but some coals of oak would remain by early morning, which helped keep the chill out of the kitchen. During a spell of cold weather, the cookstove and parlor stoves would have to be tended periodically throughout the night to keep the water pipes from freezing.

To kindle a fire, the housewife

took a piece of newspaper, tore it down the center crease, and crumpled and twisted each half separately. She laid about eight twists on the grate, lighting both ends of one of them as she put it in, then loosely covered these with eight to ten 3/4-inch square sticks of split ash. Within minutes her fire had started. Now according to what she was to cook, she selected fuel for her fire bed — often white birch and maple to get her chores off to a good start. (Any birch more than 2 inches in diameter should be split to dry in the shed; otherwise, the center will rot in a year's time and its usefulness will be lost. This is especially true of grey birch.)

Once the fire bed is established, the attentive cook spends her time regulating the drafts until the stove lids and oven are heated enough for her to proceed.

Most cookstoves have four different dampers. The front damper is located to the left and below the firebox. This is the primary source of draft which allows controlled combustion. Ashes drop through the grate into the ashpit below. (It is here you can bake potatoes. Coat them with either grease or aluminum foil and turn occasionally until done.) The adjustable upper damper is called the "check." By closing the front damper and opening the check, you can cool the fire and save fuel. The regulation of the check is one way to keep a more even temperature in the oven while baking.

The stovepipe damper is the chief device for getting your fire going and, later, stopping it from burning too quickly and allowing an excessive loss of heat up the flue.

One other damper is important. This is the oven damper and is located either to the left or right of the stovepipe—depending upon the make—at the back of the stove. When this is open (as for starting a fire or cutting down the surface heat of the stove), the heat goes directly to the stovepipe; when closed, it allows heat to circulate across the top and around the oven walls before escaping through the flue. An open oven damper, therefore, spreads the heat more evenly under the surface of the lid covers.

The hottest spot on the cookstove lies between the left and center back lids in a six-lidded cookstove. When the oven damper is open, this generally shifts forward along the right ridge of the firebox. One of the great advantages of cooking on the surface of a cookstove is the cook's choice of temperature range. Results can be had instantly merely by shifting the pots backwards and forwards from hot to medium heat, far off to the right or left for warming or simmering. If the stove is equipped with a pair of warming ovens or moveable trivets attached to the metal casing around the stovepipe, the cook has handy places to set her breads to rise, keep platters and food warm, dispel the dampness from salt, and hang dish towels and mittens to dry.

Many cookstoves also boast a holding tank for water on the right. Not only is warm water available whenever the stove is going, but the added humidity is healthful and seems to temper the room's cold corners.

It is oven cooking that is the hard-

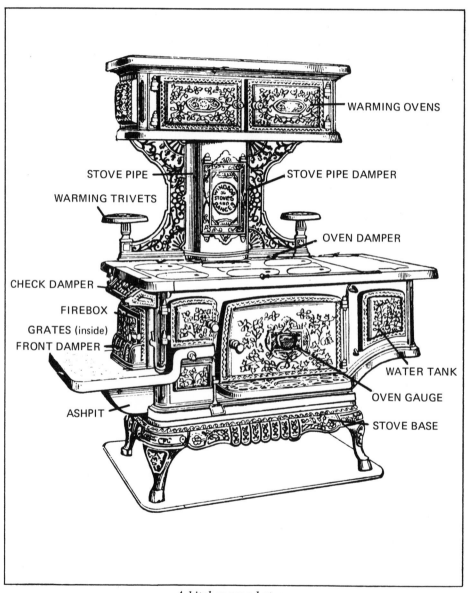

WARMING OVENS

STOVE PIPE

STOVE PIPE DAMPER

WARMING TRIVETS

OVEN DAMPER

CHECK DAMPER

FIREBOX

GRATES (inside)

FRONT DAMPER

WATER TANK

OVEN GAUGE

ASHPIT

STOVE BASE

A kitchen wood stove

est to learn and the most challenging. The art of wood-stove cooking is centered around the successful maintenance of oven temperature. Most stoves have a gauge set into the oven door. This should be treated only as an indicator of the interior temperature on most old-model stoves. Even if the needle *is* in working order, invest in a hanging oven thermometer if your experience as a cook demands more accuracy. However, by trial and error and without cost you can learn to assess the oven temperature—provided the proper kinds of wood are used in the firebox—by putting your hand in the oven temporarily. This should indicate to you whether the oven is warm, hot, or very hot (which essentially is what both the oven-door thermometer and old cookbooks will tell you anyway). Another method was to lay scraps of white paper in the oven and to judge its temperature according to the amount of time the paper took to turn brown and scorch. There are no written directions for this kind of experience.

From the stories of feasts in the days before electricity, there seems nothing that a wood-stove oven cannot do, although it takes more careful watching than modern ovens with automatic controls. Bread should be baked in a hot oven that is allowed to cool by shutting down the front damper, the chimney damper, and cracking open the check. To assure evenness (the firebox wall of the oven is the hottest side), the loaf pans should be watched and turned occasionally. If the top crust starts to brown too quickly, lay a piece of brown paper bag over the loaf. Even a soufflé—although a product of France originally and probably cooked in the more steady heat of a coal fire—can be attempted in a wood-stove oven, provided the trick of maintaining a steady temperature through the selection of wood and manipulation of the dampers is learned.

Another way of using the potential of your wood stove is to take advantage of the firebox. When the wood has burned down to coals, chop them up with a poker and level the bed. Then throw on a steak or lamb chops. Sear them on both sides and cook quickly. If applewood has been used for the fire, the results will satisfy the most discriminating taste.

Old-fashioned baked beans — costly for the modern electric stove cook—can be prepared economically in a wood stove. Leave the pot in the oven, heated by a steady-burning red oak log, and let it fend for itself all day with an occasional addition of liquid. By dinner time the beans will be ready. Meanwhile, on the stove top start soup simmering in a cast-iron pot. Add scraps of meat and vegetables from time to time for a nourishing and convenient "pot-au-feu" meal.

There are several important things to bear in mind if wood-stove cooking is to be both worthwhile and enjoyable. Keep a neat and orderly wood pile where dry stove-wood is available as needed. Clean out the ashpit and soot from around the oven frequently to reduce possible fire hazard and allow the dampers and stovepipe to function efficiently. Ashes should be kept in

15

metal buckets or ashcans at a safe distance from the house, for wood coals have surprising longevity. If kept dry, these ashes can later be used for making lye—the first step in home soap production (see page 58)—or spread on the garden to increase the potash content. Wood ashes are not much good for sprinkling on the icy walk in winter; they find their way back into the house too quickly!

Three more points should be mentioned to increase the enjoyment of using a wood cookstove. If your children are still young enough to be malleable, train them early to the onerous daily task of keeping the woodbox filled. This is a tedious but necessary process, and its neglect may result in a trip to the woodshed for a reason other than the gathering of wood.

Never use the oven as a storage closet for dirty dishes when unexpected company knocks, or for hiding valuables if you should leave the house. Human memory may not warn you to look in the oven before lighting the next fire.

Finally, if the results of cooking are to benefit both the family and the cook, clearly establish a basic rule: *only the cook* regulates the dampers while a meal is being prepared. Many a dish has been ruined and many a temper roused by a seemingly innocent fiddling with the drafts when the cook's back is turned. The best place for the non-cook—and one of the most enviable in the house—is in his rocking chair next to the stove where he can be near enough to be warm and appreciative but not get in the way.

Reference

Havens, David, *The Woodburners Handbook*, Media House, Box 1770, Portland, Me.

Keeping a Family Cow

WHEN YOU ARE PSYCHOLOGICALLY prepared to become the companion to a family cow—you will never *own* this curious rapacious beast—you will have taken a major step towards putting your home on a self-sustaining basis. For "tieing yourself down" twice a day for at least 305 days of the year to a regular milking schedule in both sickness and in health, you will be rewarded with an ample supply of whole fresh milk and milk products such as cream, butter and various cheeses, a yearly source of veal or beef, and a mountain of manure with which to enrich your vegetable garden and pasture land. The cow is the backbone of successful homesteading.

Three common breeds of dairy cow for the one-cow family are the Jersey, Guernsey and Ayrshire. The Jersey is the smallest but produces the richest milk; the Ayrshire, the largest, produces the greatest quantity of milk which has the lowest butterfat content. It is the Guernsey that is the ideal family cow.

A good Guernsey will provide more than 1000 gallons of whole milk and cream a year—enough to satisfy a family of two adults and three children, with ample skimmed milk left to feed a veal calf, a pig and a flock of chickens. An additional bonus for the spreading is more than 14 tons of manure.

Housing

Dairy cows must be kept warm, dry, and free from drafts in winter. Accommodations must be clean but not necessarily elaborate: an enclosed shelter with a window on the south side to provide sunlight, warmth and ventilation on short

17

winter days; a pen or stanchion, and an area for hay and grain storage are all that is necessary to keep your cow contented. In anticipation of the yearly calving, you should also plan space for the calf to occupy until its sale or slaughter. The cow stall should be electrified; a single bulb is safer than a lantern. It would be handy to have piped-in water, but you can always provide for her liquid needs by lugging buckets.

Pens allow the cow more freedom than stanchions but will require about three times as much bedding (hay, sawdust, or wood shavings) and more of your energy to keep clean.

The barn should be wide enough (about 6 feet) to allow you to sit and the cow to stand comfortably during milking and for her to rest during off-duty winter hours. Be sure the doors are wide enough for the expectant cow to pass through easily.

Feed, Pasture, and Water

Good milk production depends on good feed. Commercial dairy feed comes in 100-pound bags with different percentages of protein marked on the label. Prices in central New England these past few years have ranged from $5.98 to $8.48 a bag. Your Guernsey will consume three to four pounds of grain morning and night. She will also convert garden waste into milk as part of the ecological chain.

Hay has been selling from $1.20 to $1.80 a bale (40-50 pounds) at the local grain and feed store. This comes to between $90 and $100 a ton. You would do better to arrange with a neighboring farmer to deliver baled hay right from the field for less than half this amount. This saves the farmer extra labor and storage. Buying hay will save you from having to purchase expensive equipment in order to raise it yourself, or the cost of custom cutting and baling.

A Guernsey will gobble up about 15 pounds of good hay at a feeding while confined to the barn. This is about 2 tons a year. If she has good pasture of one or two acres or is staked out on the fringes of the homestead and rotated daily, feed bills will be less.

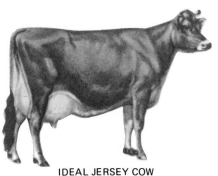

IDEAL JERSEY COW

IDEAL GUERNSEY COW

Courtesy of The Purebred Dairy Cattle Association

18

Fresh water must be available at all times as well as a medicated block of salt. In sub-zero weather the water should be warmed slightly to encourage the cow to drink.

Choosing a Cow to Live With

Once you have settled on a breed and have assured yourself that adequate housing, feed, and pasture (surrounded by three strands of barbed wire) are available, you are ready to scout around for a specific family cow. For the uninitiated, this may be the hardest decision to make. Locate a sensible dairyman in your neighborhood — one whose veracity you can trust—and pepper him with questions. As a producer, he will talk of pounds of milk; as a consumer, you will speak of quarts and gallons. Continuous high production, consistent milking and exact records are his primary concern. Yours will be steadiness, even disposition and particularly, good health.

By all means, find a registered animal that has been tested against brucellosis and tuberculosis, diseases transmittable to man. These are rarely seen in family cows today, but it is a sane precaution to take. Registered animals have been bred specifically for milk production and therefore are a good bet.

There are two ways of starting in: working up to milking by purchasing a heifer, or taking the plunge and buying a mature milker that has been bred, has already produced one or more calves, and has a good record. The former alternative has the advantage of requiring less money at the start and giving you time to warm up to the idea of being tied to a milking schedule (over the two-year period before she freshens).

Whichever way you decide, once a cow is housed on your property, your life will be changed. You must stick to your part of the bargain if she is to thrive and produce.

Milking

To learn to milk by hand is a frustrating business but one that can be mastered with patience and persistence. The basic problem is that a cow has four quarters filled with milk, and you have but two hands. You can overcome this by purchasing a milking machine that will do this job for you, but then you are left with the endless job of cleaning up—which will take you much longer.

Perfection in milking comes only with experience. Essentially it is necessary to trap the milk in the teat by pulling down slightly with the thumb and index finger, blocking its escape back into the udder, working the milk down progressively with each curled finger, and forcing it out the end of the teat with

IDEAL AYRSHIRE COW

19

pressure from the little finger against the palm of the hand.

Textbooks state that a cow lets her milk down for seven minutes as the result of a combination of circumstances which assure her all is well. These include feed, washing her udder with warm water (with a touch of bleach), and a gentle manner. If all signals are "go," she will start to produce a hormone called *oxytocin*. Loud noises, strangeness or hurry may replace this with *adrenaline* and the flow of milk will stop.

At the start it may take you 40 minutes or more to empty the bag. Both you and the cow will be snappish and tired by this time. However, with practice on your part and patience on the part of the cow, the time will be cut considerably and, while you may never match the textbook record of seven minutes, you should be able to complete the job in about ten minutes. Milk morning and night. Work with and receive instruction from a farmer for several days before actually taking over your cow's milking schedule.

The udder should be emptied at each milking and the teats stripped with thumb and index finger to prevent them from clogging with dry milk. Generally it is best to milk at 12-hour intervals, but your schedule and the changing seasons will determine this. Although slight variations from time to time will be tolerated, the cow should be milked at the same times every day.

Even though you have a tested cow and wash her udder before and after each milking, it will be necessary to take extra precautions in dealing with your milk containers. Commercial dairy suppliers sell cleansing products. However, as a homesteader with one cow, you can do a safe job of keeping your utensils clean by first rinsing them in cold water, then washing and scrubbing them with soap, bleach, and a stiff vegetable brush. Finally, rinse and scald them in very hot water and allow them to drip dry.

Breeding and Calving

The most challenging part in the yearly cycle of keeping a cow is judging when she should be bred. The presence of other cows in a herd give the most reliable indication of a cow's heat cycles. Without them you will have to rely on a combination of observation, folklore ("her ears twinkle") and guesswork. Signs to look for are a sudden slackening in production (often by as much as half), a drastic change in personality (restlessness, bellowing, general rebelliousness), spots of blood at the vulva, flank licking, a glazed expression, and an unusual amount of tail switching. If any or all of these symptoms are present and it is about 50 days after she has calved, it will be her second solid heat period and time to call the inseminator.

Artificial insemination—one of the wonders of modern husbandry—is the only method of breeding that makes sense for today's homesteader. It allows you to choose the proper mate from among the best bulls in the country for either a replacement or a beef animal. Here it costs $7.00 for the first service,

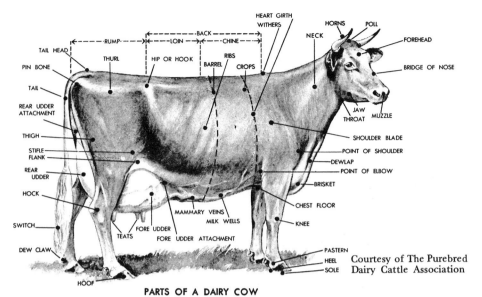

PARTS OF A DAIRY COW

Courtesy of The Purebred
Dairy Cattle Association

nothing for the second attempt, and $3.00 for a third insemination if the previous two fail.

This means, if you are raising milk-fed veal and can do the slaughtering and butchering yourself, you will be producing prime meat at home for 4¢ to 7¢ a pound!

Nine months after your cow is bred she will produce a calf. Some four to eight weeks before this, she should be dried up (either by stopping milking altogether or by skipping milkings and taking less and less milk each time she is milked) so she can devote her feed and energy to producing a creditable offspring. For most dairy cows calving is routine, especially if she has produced one or more calves already. If any hitches—such as an extended labor period or abnormal presentation—should occur, call a vet. Otherwise relax and let the cow do what instinct demands. The calf will monopolize the first milk, or colostrum, for several days. This is not fit for humans but is loaded with natural antibiotics necessary for the calf and may be colored with blood.

Ways of Coping With the Milk Supply

You can pasteurize milk on the stove by improvising a large double boiler. Heat water in the outer container until the milk in the inner one reaches 145° F. Keep it at this temperature for 30 minutes. Cool it by substituting cold water in the outer container. When the milk has reached 70° F., refrigerate it.

Cream will rise by itself and can be extracted by skimming the top of the container after a day or more of refrigeration. Using a manual or electric cream separator will hasten the job and increase the amount, but cleaning and scalding its intricate parts may not be worth the time saved.

Once you have cream, you can use it to make butter. Churning is the process which brings together the fat particles. Home churns are of the barrel, dasher, swing or box types. An electric mixer or home blender can be used instead. Cream kept in the refrigerator for two days will churn faster than very fresh cream. Cool it (46° F.-50° F.) and do not

21

fill the churn or blender more than halfway. When the butter has come, draw off the buttermilk and substitute an equal amount of cold water. Wash the butter until it forms a mass, and the water is no longer milky. Salt to taste, put the butter in a wooden bowl, and work it with a wooden spoon or your hands until the salt is incorporated and all excess water removed. Mold in a butter press or pack in a jar with a cover.

A gallon of milk will yield about 1 pound of cottage cheese. The traditional way to start cottage cheese is to set fresh skimmed milk out to sour and curdle naturally. However, for more uniform (and less acid) results, start with 1 gallon of pasteurized skimmed milk and add 1/4 cup fresh cultured buttermilk. Set the milk container in a larger container of water and heat to 72° F. Do not stir. Leave undisturbed for 15 to 24 hours until the curd forms and a watery substance (whey) appears on the top and round the rim. When the curd breaks smoothly when cut with a knife, you are ready for the next step. Hold a long-bladed knife vertically above the curd and slice through it from one side of the container to the other in 1/4-inch strips. Then turn the container a quarter turn and slice again so the result is roughly 1/4-inch squares. Now place the container in a larger pot of water on the stove and heat it slowly to 110° F. in about 30 minutes. Keep the curds at this temperature and stir frequently until they are firm. Drain off the whey, pour the curds into a colander lined with cheesecloth and let drain into a large pot or other container. Finally, draw the corner of the cheesecloth into a kind of bag and immerse this in a bowl of cold water to rinse off the remaining whey and cool the cheese. Salt to taste (about 1 teaspoon per pound). Creamed cottage cheese may be made by adding about 6 tablespoons sweet or sour cream per pound of curds.

These are only a few of the ways you can use surplus milk in your kitchen. You can also make creamed cheese, ice cream and—with more experience—hard cheeses to fill your pantry shelves.

References

Keeping livestock and using home-grown products will necessitate all kinds of reference books and pamphlets, many of them available from the U.S. Department of Agriculture or your County Agent. Here are some you may find useful if you're keeping a cow:

Cohan, Ray, *How to Make It on the Land*, Prentice Hall, 1972.

Rate, Hank, "The One-Cow Family Meets the One-Family Cow," *The Mother Earth News*, No. 15.

Stamm, F. W., *Veterinary Guide for Farmers*, Hawthorn Books.

Hobson, Phyllis, *Making Homemade Cheeses and Butter*, Garden Way Publishing, Charlotte, Vt.

Radke, Don, *Cheese Making at Home: The Complete Illustrated Guide*, Doubleday & Co., 1974. $5.95.

DAY LILY

DANDELION

Spring Tonic: Wild Greens and How to Fix Them

IF AN EXCUSE IS NEEDED THE FIRST balmy days of spring to get outdoors, what better one exists than foraging for your supper? Melting snows predict the end of winter, but it is the appearance of the first spring greens that finally confirms it.

Traditionally, spring greens stimulated the digestion, winter-weary from a steady diet of pies and pork, suet pudding, dried beans and maple sugar here in New England. They were also said to purify the blood, combat rheumatism, cure scurvy, gout and ague, and repel kidney stones. We know today—so conscious we are of nutrition—that greens gave essential vitamins and minerals long before they became available year round in capsule form.

Before the garden site is dry enough even to speculate about, there are many wild plants pushing up beyond the doorstep that will satisfy the appetite of both body and soul.

Dandelion greens are among the first that Yankees swear by, come spring. They are preceded slightly by cowslips and mustard greens down in Laidler's swamp, but the ubiquitous dandelion (*Taraxacum*

23

officinale) is everywhere you look. Harvesting first the dandelions that lie close at hand may help rid the lawn of unsightly foliage and blossoms. However, if you want the most rewarding plants, the lawn should be the last resort. It is better to leave that for a weeding session later in the season—or to let the plants blossom and use them to make wine —and to hunt for dandelion greens instead in the fallow garden or along the fence lines.

The slightly bitter taste of many wild greens can be minimized by choosing only the youngest and most tender plants. It can also be reduced somewhat by frequent changes of water as the greens cook, but the water-soluble vitamins will go down the drain along with cast-off water.

Many washings are essential before cooking, however, because these greens harbor more grit than most other vegetables. To dig them, use a sharp kitchen knife and separate them from their long tap root. A bit of root attached to the crown (that section of the plant from which roots, leaves, and blossom stems spring) of the dandelion is acceptable. Discard all yellowed leaves and broken stems and any outer leaves that show their age. Wash in three cold-water baths and as many lukewarm rinses. Pause long enough while dunking the greens to allow the dirt to settle to the bottom of the pan before you lift them out.

More greens are needed to satisfy the appetite than you might think. Cooking will reduce their bulk drastically, so be prepared to harvest and clean a monumental pile.

The country way of fixing dandelions is to bring 1-1/2 quarts of water to a rolling boil; enter the greens with cut-up pieces of fat salt pork and simmer them together gently for an hour or more. In the last half hour before serving, add pieces of peeled potato and finally, after tasting, salt. To serve, lift out the greens and place them in a heated bowl, arrange the potatoes on top, and surround it all by pieces of salt pork.

At this point a true Yankee, always aware of what is good for him, will drink the "pot likker" or cooking water as a tisane or mild spring tonic, for this is loaded with nutrition.

To cook dandelion greens so as to retain their shape, taste, color and nutrition, prepare them by washing and then cook, using only the water that clings to their leaves as liquid. Scatter salt among the leaves as you put them in the pot, cover, and apply low heat to wilt them slowly down. When their bulk is reduced by half, add a chopped, sautéed garlic clove and the oil (about 3 tablespoons) in which it has been browned. Stir gingerly to avoid tearing the leaves, and continue cooking until they are wilted to the bottom of the pan. Season to taste and serve.

Dandelion greens can be used for salad also. Blanch a few plants by putting inverted flower pots over them. (If no pots are available, boards or tiles will do.) Blanching reduces their natural bitterness.

To make a wilted dandelion green salad (3 to 4 servings), coarsely shred 1 quart of greens and place them in a large bowl. Cook 4 strips of bacon, diced; when crisp, remove from the pan. Add 2 teaspoons sugar to the grease, 1/2 teaspoon salt, a dash of black pepper, 1/4 teaspoon dry mustard, and 2 tablespoons vinegar and heat. Stir until the sugar has dissolved. Now pour this mixture over the shredded greens and toss with the bacon bits.

A Shaker Manifesto of the 19th century declares, "To make a good salad four persons are wanted: a spendthrift to furnish the oil, a miser to measure the vinegar, a councillor to dole out salt and spices, and a madman to toss it."

So you do not have to cook spring greens at all. Pick a tender harvest of leaves, wash, drain and dry between towels. Chop coarsely and add to a cold salad of beets, beans, carrots and other slightly cooked vegetables which have been dressed with oil and vinegar, seasoned to taste, and allowed to marinate for ten minutes or so. Toss well and serve.

Dandelion buds are good to eat and so are the crowns. These are somehow reminiscent of artichoke hearts if boiled for only 3 minutes and seasoned with salt and butter. But the amount one has to dig and prepare may be discouraging.

As soon as the dandelion sends up its first bloom stalk, your harvest of that plant is over. Of course you can still make dandelion wine from the blossoms and even continue to dig the roots out of the lawn. When washed, roasted in a slow oven until brown, and freshly ground, the roots make a passable coffee substitute.

A second spring green often sought by Yankees in a rural setting is the fiddlehead. Fiddleheads are ferns—cinnamon (*Osmunda cinnamomea*), bracken (*Pteris aquilina*), and ostrich (*Matteuccia struthiopteris*)—much fancied by the Orientals and by gourmet Yankees, who buy them as they appear briefly every spring in the city markets. Blessed is he who can recognize the fiddlehead before it uncurls its three-pronged head along stream beds and in open woods. Harvest when 6 to 8 inches tall. Fiddleheads have a delicate taste and should first be washed in salted water, then cooked from 3 to 5 minutes or until tender. Serve with butter or mayonnaise, or cool them quickly under cold water and dress with lemon juice and oil.

Day lilies (*Hemerocallis fulva*) come a little later in the spring. Now naturalized along the roadsides or left to decorate deserted farmyards, these orange lilies are so named because each blossom shrivels at day's end. Long before they have reached this stage, they will provide a delicate taste of spring—earlier than and just as welcome as the first asparagus. Cut shoots 6 inches tall directly above the roots. Remove any large leaves. The inner portions can be sliced raw into a salad or prepared like asparagus in a vegetable steamer. If this is not available, after washing simmer slightly until tender. As a vegetable, day-lily shoots can be enhanced with hollandaise, oil and vinegar or a horseradish dressing. Make the latter by combining 1/4 cup whipped cream, 1/4 cup mayonnaise, and 1 tablespoon or more grated horseradish.

Later in the season you may want to try eating the buds and blossoms of this orange lily, as they do in China and Japan. Boil them a few minutes, butter, season and serve like fresh green beans. You can also add them to soups and stews, or even dry them in an attic for winter use.

Since spring beckoned you out to forage for new tastes, thoughts of the winter diet from which you've just escaped may come back if you harvest too much of any one plant —or have met with opposition from a member of the family who would prefer vitamins in smaller doses. All these wild greens can be frozen as you freeze summer vegetables and kept for use in the winter months.

The common milkweed (*Asclepias syriaca*) is another offering of spring—a stalwart plant that seems to like attention because it soon shoots up again in clumps when you have thought it was picked out. Milkweed can be consumed at sev-

At the right stage for picking, the coiled head of the fern looks just like a fiddle or violin, and the stem will be from 2 to 5 inches long.

eral stages of growth—the shoots, leaves, blossoms and pods. In late spring, the first shoots (cut when 6 to 8 inches tall and still young enough to snap when bent) can be cooked to introduce you to the promise of even better things to come. Cook a pound of shoots, covered, in a little salted water for 10 minutes. Then drain and add butter. Serve milkweed shoots like asparagus—plain with salt, pepper and melted butter. Or cover them with mayonnaise or hollandaise and serve on toast.

If they taste bitter, try cooking them in several changes of water. Never start with cold water. This seems to fix the bitterness. Bring a small amount of water to the boil, add the shoots and simmer. Pour out the water once and add more boiling water. Cover and simmer for about 10 minutes or until tender.

The hearty milkweed grows along the roadside, in waste places, and in fallow ground and pastures. The wind-blown seeds parachute to more receptive ground and redistribute their potential every fall. It will often pop up among the cultivated vegetables and provide a welcome taste you have not bent your back to plant.

In addition to these yearly Yankee standbys, there is a host of other wild spring greens for those who yearn to search them out. Foremost is the neglected stinging nettle (*Urtica dioica*) so popular in Europe. Tradition says you will be beautiful if you eat nettles in the spring. Wear gloves while harvesting; the sting of nettles will cause

discomfort and may be followed by a red rash. Harvest shoots when they are 3 inches tall, young, fresh, and pale green. Wash in salted water and chop coarsely. For nettle soup, boil your harvest in beef stock, add pearl barley and season. As a vegetable, simmer nettles in a small amount of water, chop or rub through a sieve, add butter, seasoning and serve.

Another way to prepare nettles is to cook, drain and chop them fine. Melt 2 tablespoons butter, stir with 2 tablespoons flour. Add 1 cup milk and heat until thick. Season with salt, pepper and dash of nutmeg. Add to this mixture the chopped nettles and reheat. Thin with cream if desired. This plant is said to purify the blood.

There are many other spring plants to eat. You may find lamb's quarter (*Chenopodium album*), dock weed (*Rumex crispus*), and such other favorites as sorrel, mustard, upland cress, elder blossom and horseradish tops. Some of these could be cultivated in the garden, and most of them produce a higher level of nutrition than those plants we seed year after year and call vegetables.

References
Wiggington, Eliot (ed.), *Foxfire 2* "Spring Wild Plant Foods," Anchor Books, Doubleday, 1973.
Gibbons, Euell, *Stalking the Wild Asparagus*, McKay, 1962.
Wilder, Walter B., *Bounty of the Wayside*, Doubleday Doran, 1943.

Keeping a Small Flock of Chickens for Home Use

Despite the cost of commercial feeds, raising laying hens is an attractive project. A small flock requires little room, no expensive equipment, minimum physical exertion, yet can provide a steady supply of fresh eggs ("strictly fresh" as roadside signs eternally proclaim) and meat. Soufflés and omelettes make great meatless meals, and even a 12-egg angel cake made from scratch becomes a distinct possibility. Old hens and cockerels, culled from the flock, will put chicken on the table or in the freezer

Costs can be cut by growing some of the feed yourself and by raising your own birds to replace those culled from the flock.

You will have to remember to collect eggs two or three times a day (especially in hot weather), feed and water your flock regularly, and spread fresh litter (sawdust, wood shavings, chopped corn stalks, etc.) to absorb moisture and check the start of disease. You also must be willing to study chicken habits and note any sign of abnormal behavior or sickness so as to assure your investment. Unless well fed and content, chickens can quickly turn cannibalistic. They begin by pecking at the weakest or youngest and soon are having an orgy of chasing and bullying with the first bloodletting.

The homesteader has more choice in housing his flock than the commercial poultryman, whose thousands of birds are isolated in individual wire cages and must produce or go. He may confine his small flock to a house all year or erect a yard to which the hens can retire on sunny days to scratch and take

NEW HAMPSHIRE HEN

BARRED PLYMOUTH ROCK HEN

WHITE LEGHORN HEN

dust baths. Many prefer this to either complete freedom or utter isolation. Although hens left free to wander will have a more varied and interesting diet, they will cause havoc in the garden and problems on the lawn just where you may want to sit or amble barefoot.

The small family flock consists of from 6 to 20 hens. Permanent quarters can be in a partitioned-off section of the garage or barn. Or you can build a separate house. This should be constructed to make maintenance easy. It should face south for warmth and sunlight, be free from drafts and invasion by predators. Each bird should have 3 to 4 square feet of floor space. There should be one nest for every five hens, along with feeding hoppers, water, and roosts. A low-watt electric light bulb will help prolong

the day during winter months and keep production figures constant.

You can purchase chickens at various stages of development. Mature laying hens can be bought from commercial poultrymen when they are installing replacements. Or you can buy pullets that are about to start laying. These will be from 20 to 26 weeks old, depending on the breed. Day-old chicks can be mail-ordered from hatcheries and must be kept about 6 months before eggs can be expected. Many prefer to hatch replacements themselves. This can be done in a variety of home incubators on the market. Chickens take 21 days to hatch. If there are children in the farmstead, an incubator with glass panels will provide a worthwhile experience for them.

To keep a steady annual supply of future layers coming, you can let

29

nature take its course. This costs nothing and only requires the co-operation of a broody hen (one whose mothering instincts compel her to retire to the nest for a sedentary life) and the sometime presence of a rooster. "Broodiness"—the instinct to sit on eggs until they hatch—has largely been eliminated from modern cross-bred hens. However, bantams, which are only seasonal egg producers, seem to enjoy spending long weeks on a nest. Therefore, bantam hens are often kept in farm flocks to sit on eggs, their own and others.

Whether or not a rooster is kept with the flock is largely a matter of personal choice and zoning regulations. Of course, for fertile eggs he is essential. But hens lay eggs without him, and often he has been eliminated through the mistaken notion that blood spots in egg yolks betray his presence.

Tending young chicks is not difficult, nor must it be elaborate. Buy starter feed from the grain store and make sure the chicks have plenty of water and warmth. The latter can be provided by confining them to a cardboard box under the wood stove or suspending a shielded 40-watt bulb above the box. Then, when they have feathered out, the heat can be decreased gradually by raising the bulb and after 6 weeks they can be switched to growing mash.

Mixed ages are incompatible in the chicken house. Therefore, until they can take care of themselves, young pullets should be segregated from older hens. This will mean more partitions in the hen house or separate quarters and yard.

If you prefer white eggs, choose one of the Mediterranean types of chicken—the White Leghorn is still the most popular. Asiatic breeds such as Brahmas and Cochins are noted for meat production. Birds developed in this country tend to be dual purpose: producers of both meat and brown eggs. These include the Rhode Island Red, Barred or White Rocks, and New Hampshires. There are also many hybrid crosses which it would pay to investigate.

When buying day-old chicks you will have to specify pullets or straight-run (a mixture). The latter are less expensive and the cockerels can be segregated and raised as broilers (8 to 12 weeks and not more than 2-1/2 pounds), fryers (14 to 20 weeks and from 2-1/2 to 3-1/2 pounds), or roasters (5 to 9 months and weighing more than 3-1/2 pounds). Capons are emasculated cockerels and are grown for 6 to 10 months.

Once egg production starts, attention to daily care is one of the requisites for keeping it going. Water and feed should be available at all times. Unless you have a water heater in the chicken house, you will have to provide hot water from the tap during the winter. Fresh litter gives the hens something to do other than pecking at each other. They will scratch up the litter in idle hours in a constant attempt to rearrange it. Clean out the droppings frequently. Hen manure is a potent fertilizer and should be allowed to age before being spread on the garden.

The laying flock should be culled regularly to eliminate hens that are not producing or are laying at such a slow rate as to make them an economic liability. Learn the signs indicating the end of productivity: shrunken and scaly combs; strong yellow coloring of leg shanks and beaks; decreasing distance between pelvic bones. An aged hen contributes nothing but an appetite. She may live to be 8 or 9 years old but other than as a curiosity there will be no return for keeping her. Fowl—anything more than a year old—make excellent fricassees, pies, soups, and roasts if properly steamed before they are baked.

Unfortunately, chickens have the habit of molting, or dropping their feathers periodically. They are nonproductive while waiting to fluff out again. This may last from a few weeks to several months. A change in the feed, temperature, length of daylight, lack of water, or just orneriness seem to precipitate a molt.

If you keep good laying hens through their molt, they will resume production. If erratic or frequent molting occurs, the hen should be marked for the pot and dispatched quickly.

Feed (mash or pellets) can be supplemented by strewing vitamin-rich garden wastes in the chicken house or run. Hens also relish soured milk, which adds calcium for the formation of harder egg shells, and table scraps. Of course, the homesteader with land and equipment should earmark patches of fodder corn, small grains, etc., for his chickens when he plants in the spring.

Because egg production will dwindle and stop during a molt, take steps to preserve eggs during times of strong supply. To test an egg for freshness, float it in a glass or pan of water. The freshest will sink first. Those that float are ques-

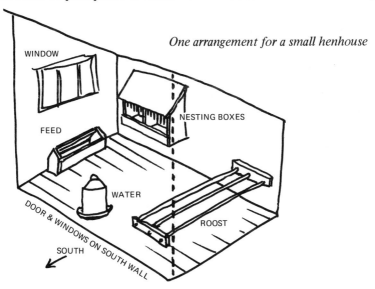

One arrangement for a small henhouse

WINDOW

FEED

NESTING BOXES

WATER

DOOR & WINDOWS ON SOUTH WALL

SOUTH

ROOST

tionable—or worse. Eggs deteriorate rapidly and will absorb unpleasant odors, especially if they have been washed and scrubbed. This opens the pores in the shell and allows air to penetrate and decay to begin.

A cool cellar with high humidity (about 72% to 80%) is a good place to store eggs for several months. A glut in late spring and early summer can then be used in the early fall. Old-timers sometimes preserved their surplus by packing eggs in sawdust, small end down. Or they applied a protective coating of oil or grease and packed the eggs in bran and salt. One cookbook of the past century suggests using lime water for keeping eggs. This is done by mixing a pound of slaked (hydrated) lime in one gallon of boiling water. When cold, the mixture is poured over eggs in a jar or crock. Place a saucer on top to keep the eggs submerged. Store in a cool place. Renew the lime water every three weeks.

Another method popular today is to use water glass. No renewal is required. A quart can of this commercially prepared product can be bought in a country or hardware store. Mix 1 part water glass in 11 parts water. Use an earthenware or metal 5-gallon container and place the eggs in solution—again, pointed end down—leaving 2 inches of liquid covering the eggs. This recipe will keep about 16 dozen eggs. Store in a cool place and cover well to prevent the solution from evaporating. The eggs will be good for up to six months; after that the shells become brittle.

To use water-glass eggs, wipe the shells clean but don't wash them. The solution will turn jelly-like after a time but will still be a good preservative. Eggs may be added to or withdrawn from the water glass at any time. Some suggest that water-glass eggs cannot be boiled. However, if the shell has not become too brittle, prick the large end with a pin before boiling to prevent the shell from bursting.

A final method of treating eggs for storage is to dip each one in boiling water for 5 seconds and allow it to cool. Submersion at a more moderate temperature (130° F.) for 15 minutes also will coat the shell with a thin layer of coagulated albumen and slows down the rate of deterioration. Treated this way and stored in a cool place with about 80% humidity, eggs should keep several months.

A final word about keeping a small flock of chickens is in order. Select a common breed and give your flock regular attention if you expect returns in eggs and meat. Start small. It is better to have a handful of hens in good production than a houseful of voracious appetites.

References
Raising Livestock on Small Farms, Farmer Bulletin 2224, U. S. Department of Agriculture.

Rice and Botsford, *Practical Poultry Management,* John Wiley & Sons, Inc., N.Y.

Seven Ways to Greater Egg Profit, Leaflet 327, U.S.D.A.

Kains, M.G., *Five Acres and Independence,* Pocket Books, 1948.

Whole Wheat Bread from Grain to Loaf

WATCH YOUR KNUCKLES AND YOUR back as the swiple arcs the air. Flailing is only one of the acquired arts you will have to master when making whole wheat bread for the homestead from seed to loaf. But—like chopping wood—it serves a double purpose. Flailing separates grain from straw while preheating the appetite in anticipation of one of the most welcome aromas to pervade the kitchen. The odor of fresh baked bread alone is worth the effort of preparation; a thick slice of whole grain bread hot from the oven, capped by a melting slab of butter, certainly stands as one of the most delicious foods of all time.

In times past, general farms throughout New England raised small grains—wheat, rye, barley and oats—most of which were used to feed stock. Flour for home use was ground locally, but as labor became scarcer and mills closed, the practice died. Few millers ply their dusty, noisy trade along the waterways of New England today. Yet some still stone-grind grain and supply gourmet shops, natural food stores, and discriminating cooks.

Many kinds of wheat are grown for flour. Although sources suggest planting the variety that is successfully grown in your area, with grain-growing for home use only now experiencing a rejuvenation in much of New England, the best procedure is to experiment. Even county agents hereabouts admittedly lack the experience to offer sound advice.

Winter wheat is so named because it is sown in early fall several weeks before the first killing frost. It germinates and grows but remains dormant under winter snows. In spring

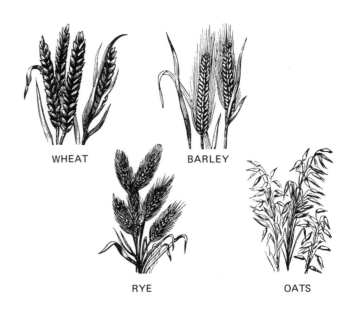

WHEAT

BARLEY

RYE

OATS

it greens again and develops until harvest time in early summer. Spring wheat is sown as early in the spring as the ground is workable and harvested before the advent of hot weather.

Hard red winter and hard red spring wheats are used primarily for making bread. Soft red winter wheat is used for cake dough and pastries. Generally, flour made from the hard wheats will rise better and take heavier handling.

Despite the preference for spring wheat by bread makers, here in New England it would be better to plant soft red winter wheat as a first experiment in growing your own grain. In case the crop fails to develop properly because of local soil and climatic conditions, you will at least have gained a cover crop to check erosion and can plow it under as a green manure to enrich the soil come spring.

This variety has been grown successfully by Samuel Kayman, an organic farmer in the upper Connecticut Valley. He seeded an acre of prepared land and harvested 450 pounds of wheat, which he claims is a disappointing yield. After the seed was broadcast, it was raked or disced into the soil. Wheat will tolerate a wide pH range (a scale to determine the acidity or alkalinity of the soil) but must be planted in fairly fertile soil and be well drained.

Two bushels (about 120 pounds) will plant an acre. Before you begin your experiment, however, consider the labor and time necessary to harvest your crop—particularly if there is no local custom combine or miller

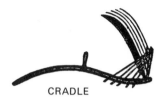

CRADLE

HARVESTING GRAIN

to convert your harvest into flour. According to Kayman, one-eighth of an acre—or an area about 50′ x 100′ —will provide enough wheat for an average homesteading family. For this about 15 pounds of seed will be necessary.

Small grain seed is available through farm supply houses or natural food stores but rarely is listed in commercial seed company catalogs. (See list which follows.)

There are two principal methods of harvesting small grains. Large operations in the wheat-growing country of the Midwest use a combined harvester-thresher. But these are hard to locate to service small plantings in oddly-sized Yankee fields. Probably you will have to revert to old-fashioned methods by cradling your harvest.

A cradle is a scythe furnished with a set of long, parallel fingers for catching the grain as it is mowed and laying it in swaths. If a cradle is not available, an ordinary grass scythe can be used but the wheat will have to be hand-gathered to bundle and stack.

For home-use, wheat is cradled before it is fully ripe, bound into bundles, stacked in sheaves, and allowed to stand in the field three or four days to completely ripen. Then it can be carried to a dry shed and left to "sweat" a few weeks or until you are ready to flail it.

A flail is an ancient farm instrument—once even converted into a weapon of war—that consists of two wooden parts: a long handle and a shorter, stouter stick called a *swiple* or *swingle*. These are usually hinged

35

with leather thongs to allow the swiple to swing freely. As it arcs back, hopefully the knuckles of the flailer will be out of the way as he grasps the longer handle.

Flailing is usually done on a clean sheet on the barn floor or outdoors on a dry day. The wheat is beaten to separate the stalk or straw from the berry (seed).

After the seed is collected, it is winnowed on a breezy day by pouring it repeatedly from one container to another until the chaff is blown away and the heavier seed falls into a receiving bucket.

When this operation is complete (and the straw set aside for bedding down the stock), store your harvest in a dry, mouse-proof place until ready to be ground. Grind in small amounts as the need arises. Much of the nutritional value is lost if the berry is ground prematurely or if it is exposed to high temperatures.

There are several kinds of home

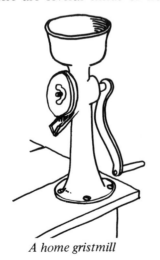

A home gristmill

grain grinders available. Hand-operated grinders—Corona and Quaker City among them—average in price from $12 to about $30. Electric mills, of course, are more expensive. These cost from $95 to $245 for a large-capacity mill capable of grinding 100 pounds of flour in an hour.

For the amounts needed in most home kitchens, either a hand grinder or a common electric blender will be sufficient. The latter will grind wheat berries into a coarse but usable flour quickly. Generally 1 pound of berry will yield a little more than 3 cups of flour.

The beauty of the hand grinder—with either metal or carborundum "stones"—is that it can be adjusted so as to regulate the fineness of the flour through successive grindings. A wing nut keeps the stones at set distances. Unlike the water-powered mill stones of old, these will not have to be redressed to keep grinding effectively. Many prefer coarse ground wheat for bread; it provides a nuttier flavor, a crunchier texture. Others want a smoother, finer flour. Your choice really depends on the recipe and personal preference.

Here are three recipes for whole wheat bread, all tasty and nutritious and well worth the effort of growing your own grain.

Baking bread is an art. Whether you make a loaf at a time or enough to supply your family's needs for a week at one baking, the results will depend on a set of variables such as the quality of the ingredients, the temperature and the humidity. If your first attempts are not too successful, or if your results seem to take a slump after several good batches, try again. Make all conditions as close to perfect as possible. Only experience will bring perfection.

The first introduction to bread-making may be in watching instinctive cooks practice their magic. One remembered recipe—taken at the elbow of the wife of a Newfoundland fisherman—uses terms such as "butter the size of an egg" and "a well worn sweat shirt" to cover the rising dough. The problem she did not experience was how to remove sticky dough from hairy arms. (Add more flour while kneading the dough.)

Another instinctive cook is Mrs. Scat, a frequent visitor. She adds ingredients by "feel." The following recipe is adapted from watching her. It has been translated into more literal terms to produce an excellent loaf with very little work.

Mrs. Scat's No-Knead Whole Wheat Bread
(one loaf)

4 cups freshly ground whole wheat flour
2 packages dry yeast (2 tablespoons)
2 tablespoons molasses
1-3/4 cups warm water
1/4 cup cooking oil
1 tablespoon salt

Put 4 cups freshly ground whole wheat flour into a mixing bowl and place it in the oven to warm. The heat should be as low as possible. In a gas oven, the pilot light will do. Proof the yeast (to assure its viability) by dissolving the yeast in 1/2 cup warm water. If after a few minutes it does not bubble, throw it away and start with a new batch. Add 2 tablespoons molasses to active yeast and stir. Meanwhile, grease a 9″ x 5″ x 3″ bread pan with oil, butter or lard. Add flour, 1/4 cup oil, 1-1/4 cups water, and 1 tablespoon salt to the yeast and molasses. The resulting dough should be sticky. If too liquid, add more flour. When it is thoroughly mixed, spoon the dough into the pan, distributing it evenly, especially in the corners. Put the pan in a warm place to rise and increase in size by about 1/3. Bake in a 450° oven about 40 minutes.

(One hint for slicing hot bread successfully is suggested by Louise Dickinson Rich in *We Took To The Woods*. Preheat your bread knife on the top of the stove before slicing.)

Another dependable recipe comes from *Beard on Bread*,© 1973 by James A. Beard, reprinted by permission of Alfred A. Knopf, Inc. This recipe originated at the Norwegian Government School for Domestic Science Teachers.

Whole-Meal Bread With Potatoes
(two round loaves)

2 packages dry yeast (or 2 tablespoons)
1/2 cup warm water
1 pound peeled and grated potatoes
3 cups buttermilk
1 tablespoon salt
6 cups whole-meal whole-

wheat flour (about 2 pounds berry)

4 cups all-purpose flour

Proof the yeast in warm water. Heat the potatoes with a small amount of buttermilk, then add to the yeast. Add the salt and the rest of the heated buttermilk. Stir in all the flour, a cup at a time, until the dough is firm. Knead until elastic. Place in a buttered bowl and cover. Let rise until doubled in bulk. Now punch down the dough and knead again. Shape into two round loaves and place on a buttered baking sheet. Again let them rise until doubled in bulk. Bake in a pre-heated oven at 375° until done (30 to 35 minutes).

Finally, for those who want a sweeter whole-grain bread, try this:

Whole Wheat Bread With Honey
(three small or two large loaves)

3 tablespoons butter
3 tablespoons honey
1 pint milk (2 cups)
1 tablespoon salt
2 packages dry yeast
6 cups whole wheat flour

Proof the yeast in 1/2 cup of the warmed milk. Melt butter and honey in the remainder of the milk in a saucepan over low heat. When lukewarm add the yeast and salt. Stir while adding flour until the dough is stiff enough to knead. Knead on a floured board for about 8 minutes. Put in greased bowl and let rise until doubled in bulk. Turn out on a floured board and knead again for a few seconds. Then divide into three small or two large loaf pans and let rise again. Bake in a pre-heated 375° oven about 50 minutes.

References

SEED SOURCES:

Johnny Appleseed, Acton, Mass.

Stamford Seed Co., 560 Fulton Street, Box 366, Buffalo, N.Y. 14240.

Rhorher Brothers, Smoketown, Pa.

FLOUR MILL SOURCES:

Corona Mill—Grinds corn, wheat, nuts, seeds, etc. Easily adjustable. Speedy and easy to operate. Heavy duty cast iron. Weighs about 10 lbs. $16.50 postpaid. Electric flour mills for $179.50. Write for more information: R & R Mill Company, 45 West First North, Smithfield, Utah 85335.

Quaker City Mill—Flour on one grinding. $11.95 plus postage from: Nelson & Sons, Inc., P.O. Box 1296, Salt Lake City, Utah 84110.

Lee Electric Flour Mill catalog from Lee Engineering Co., 2023 W. Wisconsin Ave., Milwaukee, Wisc. 53201.

READING:

Logsdon, Gene, "Grow Wheat in Your Garden" *Organic Gardening*, Jan. 1972.

Beard, James, *Beard on Bread* Knopf, 1973.

Raising and Drying Beans and Corn

ALTHOUGH ANY VARIETY OF BEAN and corn that matures in the garden can be dried for winter use, for best results plant those that have been especially developed for drying.

Raising and drying shell beans is one of the easiest garden projects. In addition to tasting good, beans are rich in amino acids which make up proteins and are essential to our diets. A good corn crop is more of a challenge—and will take more room in your garden—but your own home-grown, home-ground corn meal is a superb basis for fine dishes like johnny cake, polenta, and Indian pudding.

Both beans and corn are warm-weather, warm-soil crops generally planted when all danger of frost has passed. Both will need shallow cultivation at first to cut down competition from weeds. This can be done with a lightweight hoe, walking cultivator, or rototiller. Later on, you can just leave them to "vegetate" until ready for harvest.

BEANS

Bush beans are planted every 3 inches in rows that are spaced 2-1/2 feet apart. Pole beans are hilled around a supporting stake or pole and thinned to 3 or 4 vigorous plants after they have germinated. Snap beans, pole or bush, that develop beyond the pencil thickness that is the gourmet's delight (both for eating fresh and freezing) and seem to keep growing while your back is turned should generate neither panic nor guilt in the gardener. Leave them on the vine to mature completely, and you will have a whole parcel of winter meals with scarcely any effort. Or save them for next year's seed crop.

If you are going to devote a larger

part of your garden to raising beans for drying next season—a thrifty alternative in view of present supermarket prices for dried beans, until recently considered a poor man's fare—pore over seed catalogs and order beans specifically recommended for drying. These may include kidney beans, soldiers, Vermont cranberries, navy beans, limas, white pea beans, and soybeans. First, take into account the length of your growing season. Soybeans and limas have the highest protein value, but they both need a longer time to mature than is generally available in central New England. Occasionally, however, a happy combination of temperature, water, and frost-free days may produce a respectable crop.

Shell beans (another name for dried beans) are harvested when the pods have matured and begun to dry, but before they open and scatter their seeds. The gardener must achieve a happy medium in judging minimum loss from immaturity and the ultimate loss of his entire crop. The leaves of the vines will generally turn brown when they are about ready to harvest. Bush beans can be pulled and stacked in the garden to dry. If the weather is fair, they can be piled on stakes until drying is complete. The stacks must be loose enough to allow circulation and high enough off the ground to prevent rotting. Pole beans can be left where they grew until dry. If the weather at the time of harvest is damp or frosty, pile the vines on the barn or garage floor under cover until dry.

When the beans have dried (the pods will shatter and the beans will begin to lose their grip), you can either process them immediately or wait until other outside chores are wrapped up for the winter.

Small amounts of beans can be shelled by hand. If you have a large harvest, you will find it more efficient either to flail the bean pods or use a hand- or power-operated winnowing machine (the kind you often see housing petunias on rural lawns).

When farmers had commodious barns, come early fall they would sweep the central aisle, distribute the beanpods in a neat windrow along its length, and go to it with the flail. This was a farm chore young boys were encouraged to practice, for it allowed them to vent their aggressions in a positive, family way. When all the pods had been beaten effectively, they were raked away, and what was left was swept up and deposited in baskets. The sliding doors at both ends of the barn were pushed open to create a proper draft, and the harvesters turned their beans from the baskets through wire sieves into barrels. What chaff did not blow away was caught in the sieve and shaken out. The beans, now clean, were stored away to use either for eating or next year's seeds. Flailing can be done on a lawn by spreading the beans on a canvas or sheet, but the weather must be dry with a fair wind blowing.

A small winnowing machine will do the same job by creating a forced draft through oscillating wire trays as the handle is turned. The chaff is blown away and the bean seeds

Winnowing machine

shaken down to a waiting receptacle. Working models of these once common time-savers are being collected by antique buffs rather than by homesteaders.

Beans growing are subject to attack by beetles, rust, mosaic, and woodchucks; dried, they may be permeated by weevils. These parasites lay their eggs on the green pods while the beans are in the garden. They hatch into grubs which burrow through the pod into the bean. Several hatchings may occur while the beans are in storage. To combat this infestation, after drying, place the beans on screened trays in a cold oven. Heat gradually to 135° F. and hold for 30 minutes. Cool before storing. Store dried beans in airtight tin or glass containers in a dry, cool place (45° to 60° F.).

There are many ways to use your harvest in cooking. Dried beans must be either soaked overnight or parboiled before they are ready to cook. If time is essential, and you have neglected to soak the beans, cover them with cold water, bring to a boil, and boil for 1 minute. Remove from heat, cover, and allow to sit 45 minutes to 1 hour. Finally, drain and rinse in cold water. Now they are ready to cook.

Baked Beans (10-12 servings)

Each family seems to have the one and only recipe for this traditional Saturday night supper. Here is one that is worth trying: Soak overnight or precook 2 pounds (4 cups) white beans (soldier, Great Northern, or navy pea beans). Drain and put in kettle with cold water to cover. Bring to a boil and simmer gently until partially cooked. Test this by taking a few beans on the tip of a spoon and blowing on them. If the skins burst, they are ready to use. Drain. Save the liquid. Cut a 1/2-pound piece of salt pork in half and score by making cuts 1/2 inch deep. Place one piece in the bottom of a bean pot. Cover with a layer of beans. Coarsely chop 2 onions and combine with chopped parsley and 1/2 teaspoon dried thyme leaves (or 1 teaspoon fresh). Spoon some of this mixture over the beans, add another layer of beans, and repeat layering until mixture is used up. End with remaining beans and top with salt pork. Add to reserved bean liquid 2 teaspoons powdered mustard, 1 scant teaspoon ginger, 1 teaspoon salt and some pepper, 1/4 cup molasses, 1/4 cup brown sugar, and enough hot water to cover beans. Cook covered in 275° oven 6 to 8 hours or until done. Uncover for the last hour.

Navy Bean Soup

Soak overnight or precook 1-1/4 cups navy beans. Drain and place in kettle with a meaty ham bone, 1 medium onion chopped, 1 sprig savory, 1 bay leaf, 1 scant teaspoon salt, and pepper. Bring to a boil and simmer gently until tender (2-3 hours). Remove bay leaf and ham bone. Dice any remaining pieces of ham, and taste for seasoning. Garnish with chopped parsley. If a thicker soup is desired, blend or sieve some of the beans and liquid and return to soup before serving.

Three-Bean Salad

Make bean salad at least 12 hours in advance of serving. Cook until tender 1 cup each of kidney beans, Great Northern or pea beans, pinto or Vermont cranberry. Cool to room temperature and add finely minced onion, 1/4 cup minced parsley (minced green and red peppers, chopped celery; chopped hard-boiled egg may also be added). Dress with 1/2 cup vinegar, 1/2 cup oil, 1 or 2 cloves of crushed garlic, salt, and pepper. Garnish with chopped fresh parsley, savory or dill, wedges of tomato and hard-boiled egg.

Hot Cranberry Beans

To serve as a vegetable, soak or precook 1-1/2 cups dried cranberry beans. Cover with fresh, cold water and cook until tender over very low heat about 90 minutes. In 1/2 cup olive oil sauté until wilted 1 large onion, coarsely chopped, or 3 green onions, chopped. Add to beans. Season with salt and pepper, and garnish with chopped parsley.

Chili Bean Pie

Bring 1 cup water to a boil over direct heat in the top of a double boiler. Mix 1 cup yellow cornmeal with 3 cups cold chicken broth (3 bouillon cubes dissolved in 3 cups water) and add to boiling water, stirring until mixture boils. Place over boiling water in bottom of the double boiler, cover, and cook about 1/2 hour. While this mixture is cooking, sauté in 2 tablespoons oil until wilted: 1 onion, 1 clove garlic, 1 green pepper, all chopped. (If you wish to add meat, brown 1 pound hamburger also.) Add 1 can tomatoes, 1 or more cups corn, 2 cups cooked kidney beans, 1 tablespoon or more chili powder, 1 beef bouillon cube, and salt and pepper to taste. Spread the thickened cornmeal over the bottom and sides of a shallow, buttered baking dish as you would a pie crust. Add the bean filling, sprinkle with grated cheese, and bake at 350° for 30 minutes.

CORN

Flint or native corn is best for home-ground cornmeal, but the seed is unfortunately rather difficult to find. Sweet corn can be ground into meal, but this meal is stickier and not as apt to thicken properly when cooked. Old-fashioned flint corn is thought to have been inherited from the Indians in colonial times and is still grown in isolated areas from Rhode Island to Canada. Today most flint seed corn has been displaced by dent varieties from the mid-West, but it can still be found in country grain stores in northern New England, in natural food stores that sell whole grains, and among farmers who habitually save their seed from year to year.

As the name suggests, flint corn is hard when dried. Its kernels are larger than those of sweet corn and have a rounded rather than dented top. This variety grows well in the short seasons of northern New England but is not disease-resistant. Harvesting a sufficient crop is an annual challenge which can sometimes pay off. A further restriction for today's home gardener is that it should be planted at least a quarter mile from other varieties to assure a pure strain because it is open-pollinated. Flint corn comes in both yellow and white varieties. Sweet corn has a more distinctive flavor and is often ground with flint to combine the advantages of both.

Corn is planted either in rows or hills. In an area subject to winds and sudden storms, the hill method is recommended. The grouped stalks will help protect one another. Plant 5 or 6 seeds in hills 2-1/2 feet apart and leave the same distance between rows. Thin to 3 vigorous plants per hill. As you cultivate, draw loose soil up around the plants to add support to the shallow root system.

In addition to insect infestation or blight, corn is tyrannized by bird and beast at both ends of the growing season. Traditionally, extra seeds are planted in each hill to placate the crows, which will be among the first scavengers to find your corn patch. Metal mobiles, scarecrows, and prayer are about their only deterrents. Repeated plantings will be necessary if the seed keeps disappearing as soon as it germinates.

If the corn escapes this devastation, it can be subject to a worse predator the night before you intend to harvest your crop. Raccoons. They test the maturity of the corn beginning in late summer. When they judge it fully ripe, they call in their relatives and wreak havoc as they gorge themselves. Broken stalks and rubble will be all that is left. Larger plantings to insure some yield seem only to invite more of these bandits.

In former times when raccoons seemed less plentiful (probably because there was more open space on New England hill farms), corn was left on the stalk until the kernels glazed over. Then the stalks were shocked and left in the field to dry. By mid-October they were brought into the barn and neighbors were called in for a husking party. Later the cobs were stored in the crib and ground as needed throughout the winter.

You can still dry corn without a barn. Husk it and lay the cobs on a screened frame elevated from the ground in full sunlight. Turn several times a day. Either cover at night or bring indoors to prevent added moisture. When dry, store in a mouse-proof place.

An old-fashioned husking party

Or try a method the Indians used to preserve corn. Roast green corn in a slow oven for at least 1 hour. Test for dryness, then strip off the husks and silks and hang the cobs in dry storage. Unless thoroughly dry, corn will have a tendency to mold, so be sure of its condition before storing.

To turn your dried corn into meal, strip the kernels from the cobs with a knife and grind. For information on home grinders, both hand and electric, see p. 36. A blender may be used for corn also, just as for wheat.

Every family has its own favorite recipes for cornmeal (as for beans). Here are some excellent corn meal recipes that are worth trying:

Johnny Cake

Often called "journey cakes" because they could be transported for long distances, these were originally baked on a board beside the open fire. Later they were cooked on an iron griddle either on top of the fire or on a wood cookstove slowly and for a long time without being turned. Now you can bake them quickly in a fairly hot oven.

1 cup yellow cornmeal
1/4 cup sugar
1/2 cup flour
3/4 teaspoon salt
1/2 teaspoon baking soda
1 cup sour milk or buttermilk (sweet milk may be quickly soured by adding 2 tablespoons lemon juice or vinegar per cupful)

Sift the first 5 ingredients into a bowl and add sour milk or buttermilk. Stir only until just mixed. Pour into a buttered pan approximately 14" x 10". Cook 15 minutes in a 425° oven or until lightly browned around the edges.

Polenta—Italian Cornmeal Mush

2 cups cold water
2 cups boiling water
1 teaspoon salt
1 cup cornmeal

Mix the cornmeal with the cold water. In the top of a double boiler over direct heat bring the other 2 cups of water to a boil and slowly add the cornmeal mixture, stirring until thoroughly blended. Add the salt and bring to a boil. Place over hot water, cover and cook 1 hour. Serve with spaghetti sauce, meat sauce, onion gravy or other savory sauce, or with melted butter and parmesan cheese.

Or,

After cooking, pour into a shallow pan such as a jelly roll pan so that the polenta is about 1/2 inch deep. Allow to cool until thoroughly set. Cut into squares and fry in butter on a fairly hot griddle until lightly browned. Serve plain with sour cream or tomato sauce. Or place squares on a cookie sheet, brush with butter, sprinkle with parmesan cheese and cook in a 350° oven until hot and lightly colored.

Indian Pudding

1 quart milk
2 eggs, slightly beaten
1/2 cup yellow cornmeal
1 teaspoon ginger
1/2 teaspoon cinnamon
Pinch each of ground cloves
    and nutmeg
1 teaspoon salt
1 cup dark molasses

Mix the cornmeal with 1/2 cup milk. Scald the rest of the milk and add the cornmeal mixture to the scalded milk slowly, stirring constantly until smooth. Cook until slightly thickened. Remove the pan from the heat and add the rest of the ingredients. Mix well. Pour into a 1-1/2 quart baking dish, 2 inches deep. Bake at 325° for about 2 hours. Serve hot or warm with whipped cream or vanilla ice cream.

Creating Natural Dyes from Common Plants

THE TERMS "SPINSTER," "THE DIS-
taff side " "warp and woof" and
"shuttle" have been woven into our
language. So have "dyed-in-the-
wool" and "he's true blue." Today,
as long ago, the steady rhythm of
the spinning wheel and the thump
of the loom are heard in homes
throughout New England. Weavers
and spinsters are doing more of their
own dyeing. It's not hard—you can
find dye colors in many common
plants.

To begin a project in home dyeing, you need a safe source of heat,
scales, some pots, a few mordants,
a liberal supply of soft water, wool
(for this takes the dye more easily
than cotton or linen fibers), and
plant material. Goldenrod, lily-of-
the-valley, privet, sumac, marigolds
(*tagetes* variety), onions, dahlias, or
the barks and nuts of native trees

abound along the roadsides and in
the garden. Do not use beets and
other vegetables which produce ex-
otic colors while cooking; these are
stains and will quickly fade.

The time of harvest (for most
plants, just before they come into
bloom), soil conditions, and weather
all affect the color of the dye. Therefore, if you plan to dye a large
amount of wool the same color, collect more material than you think
you'll possibly need from the same
place, at the same time, and dye all
the wool at once. Harvest plants of
different kinds throughout the growing season; use them fresh or label
and dry them so you can continue
to dye during the winter months.

Natural wool can be purchased
as fleece or skeins. When buying
skeins, make sure they are not a
blend of wool and man-made fibers.

Left: *Sorting fleece before washing.*
Right: *Washed fleece drying on the line and on the lawn.* Photos courtesy of the Friendly Farm.

(The latter will not take dye evenly.) An unwashed fleece must be soaked 12 hours in very hot water. Then squeeze it out gently—never twist or wring—and wash it in a weak solution of soap. Rinse several times with hot water and spread out in a shady place to dry.

Pots should be of enamel, glass or stainless steel. You will need one large enough to hold 4 to 4-1/2 gallons of water. Because of the interaction of chemical mordants with the metal, aluminum must be avoided. Iron pots gray or "sadden" colors, but it is possible to use an iron dye pot instead of adding ferrous sulphate (see below).

You should have a scale that will measure in fractions of ounces up to a pound. (It takes about 1-1/2 pounds of wool to make a man's home-knit sweater.) Use a postal

scale to measure the 1/16 of an ounce of chemical mordants sometimes required.

Mordants make it easier for the dye to unite with the fiber by forming a chemical bridge which will fix it permanently. Although some plant material can be used without a mordant, most require one. Historically, vinegar, ammonia and caustic soda were commonly used. To produce a wider range of colors today, you should have on hand cream of tartar (potassium acid tartare), alum (potassium aluminum sulfate), chrome (potassium dichromate), tin (stannous chloride), and iron (ferrous sulphate). Purchase these from your druggist or from a dye and chemical supply house. Alum/cream of tartar is the most commonly used mordant. It brings out the soft, natural colors of the

47

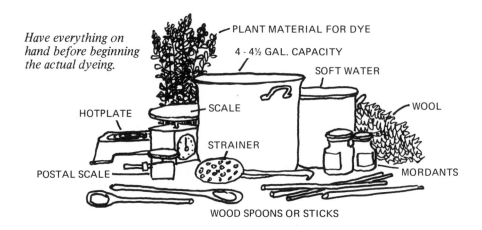

Have everything on hand before beginning the actual dyeing.

PLANT MATERIAL FOR DYE
4 - 4½ GAL. CAPACITY
SOFT WATER
HOTPLATE
SCALE
WOOL
STRAINER
POSTAL SCALE
MORDANTS
WOOD SPOONS OR STICKS

dyes. Chrome will make the colors more authoritative; tin brightens them, and iron "saddens" or grays them.

To mordant with alum, heat 4 to 4-1/2 gallons of water. Dissolve 4 ounces alum and 1 ounce cream of tartar in a small amount of water. Then add it to the pot. Immerse 1 pound wetted, clean wool in the bath and simmer for an hour, stirring the wool occasionally. Lift out the wool and press gently to remove water. Rinsing is not essential unless the wool feels sticky, in which case you have used too much alum. Adjust the amount for the next bath. The wool is now ready for the dye bath.

It is possible to mordant wool with chrome, tin or iron (use 1/2 ounce of the chemical for 1 pound of wool) as you would with alum/cream of tartar. However, tin sometimes causes the wool to become brittle. Chrome is light-sensitive, so wool pre-treated with this mordant will have to be protected from light until the dyeing has been completed.

It is better to add chrome, tin or iron as desired to alum-mordanted wool in the final minutes of the dyeing process. The wool must be lifted out and set aside while the chemical is being dissolved in the dye bath. (See directions which follow for specific amounts.)

Use wooden spoons, glass rods or smooth sticks to stir the wool. Keep all dyeing utensils and chemicals isolated from cooking equipment and out of reach of children.

Dye plants growing in New England will generally yield soft earth colors ranging from yellows through golds, greens, reds, tans, and browns to grays. They can be divided into two groups according to how they are prepared: the leaves, stems, flowers or skins of common plants, together with barks, nuts or roots, form the "fresh" group; and lichens —parasitic, flat growths that appear on rock outcroppings in the higher altitudes of New England— form the "fermented" group.

Plant material can be used either fresh or dried. You need about 1 peck (2 gallons) of stems and leaves or blossoms; 1 pound of nut shells; or 1/2 pound of roots for each pound of wool to be dyed. Dried plants can be broken and pulverized; fresh material should be shredded with a sharp knife or scissors before trying to extract the colors.

Crumble or chop the material into pieces, cover with water, and let stand overnight. In the morning bring to a boil and simmer for at least 1/2 hour to release the entire potential. Add enough water to cover the wool (about 4 gallons). *The addition of water will not dilute the dye. Once the potential has been released, it will always be available regardless of the volume of water in the dye pot.* Now heat the dye before adding wetted, alum-mordanted wool. Enter all the wool at once so the lot will dye evenly.

Directions for a specific experiment with onion-skin dye follow. You should obtain four different colors from the same dye by changing the mordant. Your colors will range from golden yellow to mossy green.

Place the dry outer skins of common cooking onions in the pot and cover them with water. Let stand overnight. You will need about 10 ounces of skins to dye 1 pound of wool, but you may reduce the amounts proportionally. (One way to collect enough of this material is to ask your grocer to save skins for you from the bottom of his bins.) In the morning boil the mixture for at least 1/2 hour. If you are dyeing fleece, enclose the dyeing material in cheesecloth and leave it in the dye

pot; if skeins, omit the cheesecloth. You can shake the wool after dyeing it, and the onion skins will drop off. Add enough water to make 4 to 4-1/2 gallons.

Yellow—Old Gold: Enter 1 pound of wet, alum/cream of tartar mordanted wool into the dye pot. Simmer for 30 minutes. At the end of this time remove 3/4 of the wool and set it aside. Continue to simmer the remaining wool about 15 minutes more. Extract this, rinse it several times in hot water until the water runs clear, squeeze and hang to dry. Alum-mordanted wool will yield colors from yellow to old gold, depending upon how long it is simmered in the dye bath.

At this point divide both the dye and the remaining wool into three equal parts. Put 1/3 of the dye into the pot for each batch.

Copper—Burnt Orange: Use chrome. Dissolve 1/8 ounce potassium dichromate in a small amount of hot water and add this to the dye pot. Enter 1/4 pound wool. Simmer 15 minutes, or until the desired color is obtained; take out the wool, rinse it thoroughly in hot water, squeeze, and hang up to dry in a shady place.

Mossy Green—Saddened Khaki: Use iron. Follow the same procedure you used with the chrome. Remember to clean the pot thoroughly after you have discarded the used dye, for you do not want any residual chemical to affect the next lot.

Bright Orange: Use tin. As above.

Each of your wool-dyeing experiments should be labeled immediately with a notation made of the mordant, date and dye material to avoid later confusion and to enable you to duplicate a specific color.

The procedure is the same for other common plants. Among these are: marigold blossoms (*tagetes* variety) for yellow, buff and old gold; spring leaves of lily-of-the-valley, greenish-yellows; privet leaves, yellow and gold; goldenrod, golds and tans; dahlia blossoms, rosy reds; coreopsis, yellows and burnt orange; bracken, soft greens; and Lombardy poplar leaves for lime yellows and golden browns.

Roots, barks and hulls from nuts of native trees often contain tannic acid. This is a natural mordant, but without additional chemicals the colors will tend towards the dark side and fading can occur. The basic procedure for dyeing is the same as above. However, the amount of soaking required to release the dye depends on the freshness of the material. If fresh, soak overnight and boil for 2 hours; if old, the material should be soaked for about a week. You can easily tell when the water starts to pick up the dye color.

The inner bark of common trees should be gathered in the spring when the sap is in the trees. If used dried, bark can be pulverized; if fresh, it should be finely chopped. A dye made from white birch bark will yield light browns. Other commonly used barks are apple (yellow-green), black willow (rose-tans with alum), spruce (tans), and black walnut (browns).

Other colors can be obtained from wood chips. Keep them separated according to tree variety and experiment for colors.

Gather butternuts in the fall while still green. Remove the hulls with a hammer (save the nut meats for the cook) and soak them. For dark tan: after 30 minutes of simmering, remove the wool, dissolve 1/6 ounce iron in the bath. Re-enter the wool and simmer with the hulls until the desired color is reached.

Cut 8 ounces of fresh bloodroot into small pieces and soak them overnight in a pot of water. Alum-mordanted wool in this dye bath will be colored a number of soft reds.

The other way of extracting dyes at home is through fermentation. For this you can use lichen. Two varieties of this parasitic plant are native to New England: *Umbellicaria pustula* and *Gyrophora dillenti*. These are potent dyes (dark reds and purple blues) which can be used over and over again without appreciably exhausting their strength for as many as ten dye lots. No mordant is necessary. They can also be used as a cold-water dye bath by simply submerging wetted wool overnight in the dye once it has been properly fermented.

Lichens grow on exposed and eroded rocks at high altitudes. They prefer moist conditions and appear to be leather-like green or olive plaques with dark brown or tan undersides. Lichens are most easily harvested when water-soaked.

Collect lichen in August and allow it to dry thoroughly. When ready to use, pulverize the plant material by rubbing it between your hands or putting it through a sieve. Place it in a wide-mouthed gallon jar with a close-fitting lid. Moisten the lichen and slowly add a solution of 1 part ammonia (non-sudsing kind) to 2 parts of water. Cap and shake vigorously. Keep it in a consistently warm place between 60° and 75° for a period of 15 to 28 days. Shake the jar every 2 or 3 days.

When ready to dye, enter wool in a cold dye bath and leave overnight. This results in a magenta or "bishop's purple." Dyeing can be repeated each night until the bath seems exhausted. But to get even more mileage from this material, heat it in an enamel pot and let it simmer 5 to 10 minutes. Enter wetted wool now and successive dyeings will produce brilliant orchid colors. When this seems to have finished off the dye, add a small amount of vinegar and enter more wool for rosy tans.

You can also grow your own dye herbs: try weld (greens and yellows), Our Lady's bedstraw roots (coral reds), wild marjoram (violets), and dyer's camomile (yellows). (See *The Forgotten Art of Growing, Gardening and Cooking with Herbs*, Yankee, Inc., 1972.)

Because a competent teacher can save you endless hours of frustration, join a dyer's workshop if there is one in your area.

References

Adrosko, Rita, *Natural Dyes and Home Dyeing*, Dover Press, NYC, 1971.

Bolton, Eileen M., *Lichens for Vegetable Dyeing* (obtainable from Robin and Russ Handweavers, McMinnville, OR 97128, or Earth Guild, 149 Putnam Ave., Cambridge, MA 02139).

Davidson, Mary Frances, *The Dye-Pot*, Rt. 1, Gatlinburg, TE 37738.

Krochmal, Arnold & Connie, *The Complete Illustrated Book of Dyes from Natural Sources*, Doubleday & Co., 1974.

Castino, Ruth A., *Spinning and Dyeing the Natural Way*, Van Nostrand Reinhold Co., N.Y., 1974.

Dye Plants and Dyeing—A Handbook, Brooklyn Botanic Garden, Brooklyn, NY 11225.

Natural Plant Dyeing—A Handbook, Brooklyn Botanic Garden, Brooklyn, NY 11225.

Brewing Apple Cider and Vinegar at Home

To MAKE NATURAL APPLE CIDER AT home today is not difficult; to try to prolong its life by storage presents a greater challenge.

Just before the first real frost, and after the choicest apples have been harvested and stored in the cellar for winter use, the windfalls and culls are collected and sorted. These stubble-spiked and bruised rejects may be less worthy to be eaten out of hand, but can be ground and pressed to make a number of beverages and enough vinegar to last the winter.

Only two pieces of equipment are needed to make apple cider: one device to crush the apples and reduce them to pomace; another to express their juice. These two functions are usually combined in one machine called a cider press, which can be purchased from a commercial

supply house, found at country auctions, or improvised with a few stout planks, several timbers, some wooden slats, burlap or cheesecloth and a car jack (see accompanying diagrams).

The commercial press will extract more juice than a homemade one because it can exert greater pressure through a hydraulic ram or mechanical screw-type press. But for home production, a one-horsepower motor can be coupled to the grinder and pressure on the pomace or "cheese" can be applied by using a jack or turning the screws by hand.

Cider apples hereabouts are best from "natural" trees—those unnamed varieties that spring up along fence lines or appear surrounded by second growth in what used to be a pasture. These have never been sprayed and may not have an attractive appearance in a commercial sense, but their apples will yield abundant juice to be converted into sweet cider. Locally we find the King, Snow Apple, and one delightfully called Sheepnose. The Baldwin is a reliable cider apple. So are more familiar varieties such as the Stark, Cortland, Northern Spy, Greening, and Delicious. Crab apples should not be used alone for they are somehow juiceless in bulk, but a few added to the pomace of other varieties will make a tangier cider.

Expect to produce about three gallons of cider from each bushel of apples. You can make cider using one kind of apple for each pressing or from several, mixed indiscriminately. The former alternative is more time consuming but will allow you to experiment with blending your own cider after the pomace is pressed and the juice put into holding containers.

The New England Farmer of October, 1823, suggests that "the worse an apple is for the table, the fitter it is for cider," and generally speaking an apple with a tough skin and a yellow flesh will yield a good beverage.

The cooler the weather, the better for making cider—provided it is not so cold as to freeze the fingers or the pomace. Cool weather retards fermentation and the late-season yellow jackets attracted by the cloying sweetness of crushed apples will be less lively.

After collecting the cider apples, wash and sort them, discarding those that are obviously rotten. Grind them (the finer the pomace the greater the amount of juice) and

spread the pomace on burlap or muslin on a slatted rack on the press. Leave enough material overhanging to enable this to be folded over the pomace and thereby contain it during the pressing. Add another rack, another layer of material and pomace, etc., until you have a stack of "cheese" layers to fit the vertical dimensions of your press. (Commercial presses are often stacked 14 layers high.)

Apply pressure slowly. Too quick a pressing will produce a cloudy cider; too much at the wrong time may rupture the fabric surrounding the pomace. (In former times clean rye or wheat straw was used as an encasing material.) The juice must be strained before it is put into storage containers to eliminate obvious impurities.

Sweet cider can be drunk immediately after pressing. But if you intend to store it, you must have clean containers and know how to arrest the fermentation process as the juice passes from the vinous to the acid stage. You may notice this change as some of the sugar changes to starch and a thin layer of bubbles appears on the surface. Soon the delicacy of taste is lost, the head increases, and the cider tastes more tangy. The alcoholic content will rise rapidly and is said to give one a "brainy" feeling. When the alcoholic content reaches its maximum (about 11%), another change sets in. This occurs as the acid stage is reached; a "mother" or stringy mass appears on the surface, and the apple juices have changed to vinegar.

Central heating and cement-

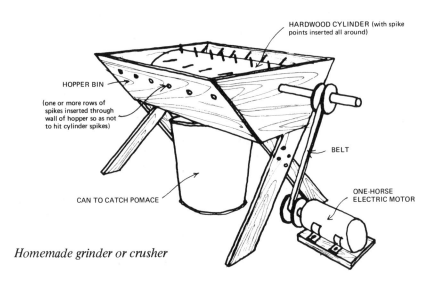

HARDWOOD CYLINDER (with spike points inserted all around)

HOPPER BIN

(one or more rows of spikes inserted through wall of hopper so as not to hit cylinder spikes)

BELT

CAN TO CATCH POMACE

ONE-HORSE ELECTRIC MOTOR

Homemade grinder or crusher

floored cellars, while making our houses more comfortable and less musty, have eliminated effective storage areas for cider and root crops.

One farm family might consume two or three barrels of cider and vinegar in the course of a winter. Cider was used as a beverage and for cooking. Vinegar was important in treating sunburn and, mixed with honey, to make a tonic. Enameled kitchenware and copper can be cleaned where burned or discolored by rubbing with salt moistened with vinegar. A tablespoonful of vinegar added to the water while cooking tough fowl or meats will save nearly two hours' boiling time. It will also remove lime spots, improve the flavor of stewed prunes, coagulate the albumen when boiling cracked eggs, and help remove lime deposits from the bottom of a teakettle when boiled in the kettle occasionally.

Wooden barrels (31-1/2 gal. capacity) and even hogsheads (2 barrels) filled with cider were handy to the cook and thirsty farmhands. Visitors would appear at the drop of a rumor to taste and compare the various stages through which the cider progressed. And young children with a clutch of clean rye straws inserted through the bunghole would be endlessly amused until expressly forbidden their pleasure by stern parents.

Today, glass and plastic jugs can be used for short-term storage. Or cider can be frozen and thawed when wanted. Chemical additives are used commercially and can be in the home to help preserve sweet cider for several weeks. Pasteurization and sealing sweet cider in glass will augment its keeping power but the resulting beverage will be apple juice rather than cider—not the same thing at all to true devotees.

You can refrigerate cider from the press at 32° to 36° F. and expect it to last one to two weeks. If you freeze

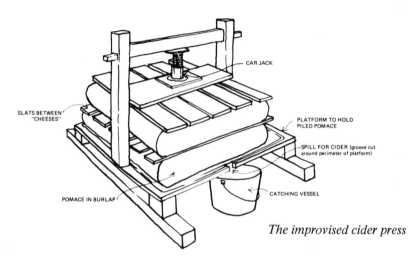

SLATS BETWEEN "CHEESES"

CAR JACK

PLATFORM TO HOLD PILED POMACE

SPILL FOR CIDER (groove cut around perimeter of platform)

POMACE IN BURLAP

CATCHING VESSEL

The improvised cider press

it (fill the container to only 90% capacity to allow for expansion), it will keep about one year. Pasteurization requires that the liquid be brought to 170° F. and held there for about ten minutes. Then it is bottled, sealed, and will last practically indefinitely. If you are determined to use a chemical additive, purchase *potassium sorbate* and add one ounce to each two gallons of cider. Mild refrigeration (50° F.) will help preserve this for several weeks.

If you can effectively store apples in your cellar and are a devoted sweet cider consumer, the best method of assuring a continuing supply without the worry of having it turn to vinegar is to make cider at intervals throughout the winter in amounts that can be consumed immediately.

But traditionally cider has been stored in stout oak barrels made from heartwood and hooped with metal bands. Barrels formerly used by whiskey makers are popular and available. Make sure your container is sweet-smelling and clean. Use a rinse of soda and water to purify the barrel, or put a pint of unslaked lime in the barrel and add three to four gallons of steaming water. Agitate and let stand until cool. Rinse with cold water and repeat if necessary. "Stumming" barrels was a common practice in the early 19th century. This was done by dipping a canvas cloth (12 inches long by 2 inches broad) into melted brimstone. When dry the canvas "match" was lit and suspended in the bunghole of the barrel and allowed to burn out. This "match" would help suppress improper fermentation and its fumes would be incorporated into any cider left in the barrel. (Additional flavoring could be added by strewing spices like ginger, cloves, cinnamon, etc., on the match before it dried).

By the 1820s the Shakers, well

55

known for their innovations, found that the slower cider is in fermenting, the better it will be. Modern cider-makers can hold fresh cider 24 to 72 hours at 40° F. to allow the sediment to settle and without danger of too fast a change. Then it is siphoned, tapped, or drained into barrels or jugs. The principal object is to stop the working as soon as the vinous fermentation is complete. Then the vessel is made airtight to prevent the escape of carbonic acid and the intake of oxygen. By mixing the proper quantity of alcohol with the cider at this stage, the Shakers and others stopped cider from turning to vinegar. Although brandy was sometimes used for this purpose, a half gallon of common whiskey added to a barrel was enough to prevent "souring." Sugar, honey, or molasses was also used, but alcohol was more favored.

Cider royal was the name applied to a beverage manufactured by the Shakers and made by boiling down fresh cider and reducing it from one-third to one-quarter of its original volume. This was not an everyday drink but reserved for holidays and special guests. It was a richer, more intoxicating beverage which also had increased keeping powers. *Boiled cider* was practically the same thing but was not so greatly reduced. This was commonly used for making apple-sauce and boiled cider pie. It was also a major ingredient of apple butter.

Cider wine can be made by reducing the bulk of fresh cider through the action of severe frost. Fresh cider is poured into wide, shallow vessels and placed where it will freeze. The ice is skimmed off the surface several times a day for two or three days; in this way the water is discarded and the spirits remain. This reduces the original bulk to one-fourth or one-fifth. It can then be bottled and kept at a moderate temperature.

Cider spirit, another Shaker innovation, was made by distilling the lees and adding one to three gallons of this to fresh cider in the barrel. This was bunged airtight and allowed to stand until mature (usually after the first of the new year).

Hard cider can be manufactured from fresh cider rather than let alone to develop at its own rate. Add one-half pound white sugar to a gallon of sweet cider. Throw in a handful of raisins, cinnamon, cloves, nutmeg, ginger, etc. for extra flavor. Bring an air tube tightly fitted to the bunghole to a container of water below. When fermentation ceases (noted by the absence of air bubbles in the water container), the barrel is sealed and stored for about two years. Fermentation in a hogshead takes about eight months. Once hard cider is exposed to air, it turns to vinegar.

Applejack is an alcoholic beverage consisting of the unfrozen core of a container of hard cider.

In dealing with cider vinegar, remember that acid is corrosive. Do not use copper, zinc, iron, or galvanized containers. The interaction of acid with these metals will produce a poison.

One method of making *cider vinegar* is to leave fresh cider in an open barrel covered with a board or cloth. After the "mother" culture forms, skim the surface before using the liquid. Another method is to add one-quarter pound white sugar to each quart of fresh pressed cider. When cool add one-quarter cake of yeast and store in a stone or glass jar with only a cloth covering; or plug a glass jar with cotton until after fermentation. In about two weeks, separate the fermented liquid from the sediment and to each quart of liquid add one-half pint of unpasteurized vinegar. Cover with a cloth, stand in a warm place until the vinegar is strong enough to use, then bottle and cork. (Just before bottling you might want to experiment with making different kinds of herb vinegar. This is the time to add sprigs of tarragon, basil, etc.).

With some or all of these by-products of windfalls stored against a long winter, you should begin to experience a feeling of plenty. Here are three more ways to use cider:

Apple Butter

Take pared, cored, and sliced apples and add twice as much boiled cider by measure. Simmer and skim until it is of a marmalade consistency. Sweeten to taste with brown sugar and add spices, if desired. This can be stored in jars or wooden pails practically indefinitely.

Shaker Cider Pie

Put one-half cup boiled cider into a saucepan and add 1 tablespoon butter, 1 cup maple sugar, 1/4 cup water, and a dash of salt. Simmer. When slightly cool, add 2 beaten egg yolks and fold in 2 beaten egg whites. Pour into an unbaked pie shell, sprinkle with nutmeg, and bake until the custard is well set and the crust brown.

Apple Mead

For a special beverage, mix fresh apple cider with an equal amount of honey. Stir until dissolved. Pour into a stone crock and cover. Let stand in a warm place for several weeks. Skim when necessary, bottle and seal.

References

Making and Preserving Apple Cider—U.S. Department of Agriculture, Farmers' Bulletin No. 2125, available from County Agents, Congressmen, or by writing directly to the Superintendent of Documents, U.S. Printing Office, Washington, D.C. 20402 (enclosing 10¢).

Piercy, Caroline B., *The Shaker Cookbook—Not By Bread Alone—*, Crown Publishers, Inc., N.Y. 1953.

Any number of household aid or cook books published at the turn of the century or before.

Making Plain and Fancy Soap

ABOUT 60% OF THE WORLD'S SUPPLY of soap is consumed in this country. This reflects our passion for cleanliness as a result of the marriage, more than a century ago, of soap manufacturers and the fledgling advertising industry.

The two basic ingredients of soap are lye and fat. Lye can be manufactured at home by dripping water through wood ashes in an ash pit or open-ended barrel. Or you can purchase commercial lye in the local supermarket. Animal fats saved from cooking or home butchering or bought from your meat man all make good soap. Vegetable oils (olive, linseed, coconut, etc.) are becoming common in natural food stores, and vegetable shortenings (Crisco, Spry, *et al.*) have been available at grocery stores for years.

In the horse-and-buggy era of a hundred years ago soap was soap, without fancy frills. Its color varied from pale yellow to tan, largely depending on the age of the fats used. It smelled like soap, with a slight overtone of fat, and it performed with a vengeance when used to scrub clothes and wash dishes. Sometimes the housewife would make a smaller batch of scented soap (using herbal decoctions like lemon, lavender, or rosemary) for the wash basin in the guest room or to caress more tender skin. Yet it was the homemade bar soap that she depended on.

Soap making usually took all day and had to be done outdoors in a large kettle, sometime after butchering and before the weather warmed. Wood ashes were collected from stoves and fireplaces and dumped into the ash pit. This might be

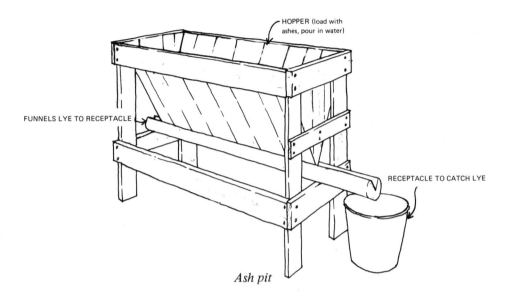

HOPPER (load with ashes, pour in water)

FUNNELS LYE TO RECEPTACLE

RECEPTACLE TO CATCH LYE

Ash pit

simply an open-ended barrel set on a slanting board. More often it was an ash pit specifically constructed for lye making. Made of stout oak planks, it was built in a "v" shape some 5 to 6 feet long and about 4 feet high, with a trough (made by nailing 2 six-foot boards together in a "v" form) along the bottom to channel the lye and lead it to a holding receptacle (see diagram). Straw lined the bottom of the pit to prevent the ashes from seeping through. With the ashes loaded, water was poured in from the top, and when it had trickled through as lye and was stored in a stone crock or wooden barrel, one of the ingredients for making soap was ready. Chemists know this product as potassium hydroxide or caustic potash.

Meanwhile, animal fats (bacon drippings, pork rind, suet and trimmings from late fall butchering) had all been hoarded for the annual soap-making day. Beef fat (tallow) is still the principal animal fat used and will produce the hardest soap. But mutton fat, pork fat (lard), and even goat fat were all commonly used. The fat was thrown into the iron kettle over a brisk fire outdoors and rendered (reduced to liquid form by melting).

Then the lye was added, and the whole mess stirred until it acquired the consistency of honey or jelly. The soap was poured into molds or flat trays and allowed to harden and age.

Soft soap was made by stopping the boiling process early. The soap was stored in stone crocks or barrels in the cellar and dipped out when needed for laundry. Often a small wooden bucket of soft soap (or a coconut hull with the top cut off) was left near the kitchen sink for doing the dishes. This was a liquid soap long before the days of the ubiquitous plastic squeeze bottle—fierce stuff on both hands and clothes—but effective.

To render fat safely in the kitchen today, the fat should be first finely divided, preferably by putting it through a meat grinder, then placed in a rather flat pan, and put in a moderately warm oven (250° to 300°, no higher). The entire rendering should take no more than half an hour. The liquid fat can be poured off every ten minutes or so to make it easy to handle. Not all of the fat will render, and what doesn't is called "cracklings" and can be nibbled, used to make crackling bread, squeezed out or discarded. Strain the liquid fat through several layers of cheesecloth to remove any impurities.

Lard and tallow will keep nearly indefinitely if refrigerated or sealed in a canning jar and stored in the cellar. Or you can make your soap the same day you render the fat.

When the lye is ready and the fat rendered, you are ready to begin. Commercial lye (sodium lye or caustic soda) can be bought under various labels at the grocery store. Be sure to buy *flake* lye, not one of the by-products.

Use only enamel or stainless steel containers when working with lye. Chemical reactions will cause aluminum, tin, or iron pots to corrode or rust. Stirrers should be either glass or wooden. Protect your hands with rubber gloves.

In making soap with homemade lye, you will find some recipes merely state to combine the two principal ingredients. This means to add the lye to the fat. The measure of success depends on the slowness of the combining and the temperature of each ingredient (between 90° and 98° F.). Women who have been making homemade soap all their lives feel the outsides of the containers as a way of testing the temperatures. Then they can heat or cool either one accordingly. Lacking such experience, use a thermometer until you get the hang of it.

The use of commercial lye, a potentially dangerous substance, requires temperature control for safe and successful results. The directions on the can of one popular brand of flake lye spells out the fat/lye temperatures specifically:

Sweet lard or soft fat:
    85° F.—lye solution at 75° F.
Half lard, half tallow:
    110°—lye solution at 85° F.
All tallow:
    130° F.—lye solution at 95° F.

Always add the lye to the fat in a thin, slow stream, stirring constantly. Otherwise, "No Soap," an expression of negation which came from seeing the mess either curdle or refuse to jell. Stir slowly for 10 to 20 minutes until the mixture is as thick as honey. Then pour it into molds.

Here is one way of making a hard, white soap:

The ingredients are 6-1/2 pounds of rendered fat, 1 can of commercial lye, and 1/2 cup sugar, which makes the soap lather. (In former times small amounts of borax, kerosene and ammonia were all added to increase the cleansing power of the soap.)

Clarify the fat by boiling it with an equal or larger amount of water in a large pail or stock pot. This will remove the salt and other impurities. Pour off the fat and discard the sediment.

Dissolve sugar in 1 cup very hot water. Add this to 4 cups warm water. Now empty a can of lye slowly into the mixture and stir. The lye will heat up on contact with the water. Since it will cause fumes, this should be done either *outdoors* or in a *well ventilated* kitchen. It is also a good precaution to have a glass of water and vinegar on hand to sip to stop coughing, or, should some splatter on your skin, to bathe the irritated area. *Keep lye out of reach of children*; caustic soda can be fatal if swallowed.

As the temperature of the lye mixture reaches that specified, pour it into the fat in a fine stream, stirring constantly. When the mixture approximates the consistency of honey, pour the liquid soap into a shallow pan or cardboard box (like a shoe box) that has been lined with a cloth wrung out in cold water. Score the soap with a knife when slightly hardened. When set, cut into squares, remove the soap from the mold and store.

You can double or triple your ingredients depending on how much soap you want to make in one batch.

Some home soap makers cover the molded soap with layers of blanket to help control the cooling and hardening process. Others find it just as effective to slide the newly made soap under the wood stove. When blanket layers are used, the soap may take several days or weeks to harden. Under the stove, soap made one day should be ready to use or store the following evening.

Mrs. E. A. Howland, writing in *The American Economical Housekeeper* in 1852, suggests collecting 10 pounds of potash and 20 pounds of grease. Clarify the grease. Then put one pail of soft water into the potash and let it stand about 1-1/2 hours. Strain the hot grease into the potash, stirring well and often. More potash will make the soap stronger. If too strong, temper it with soft water before it jells.

You can make saddle soap by using 6 cups tallow, 1 cup lye and 2-1/2 cups water. Heat the tallow to 130° F. Dissolve the lye and cool it to lukewarm. Combine tallow and lye. Stir. Just before molding, add 1 cup glycerine to enrich the mixture.

Try making a luxury soap like the following. You will need 1 pound of canned shortening, 1 cup pure olive oil, 1 cup peanut oil, 1/2 cup plus 2 tablespoons lye, 1-1/3 cups water and 3 tablespoons scented oil (see: *The Forgotten Art of Growing, Gardening, and Cooking with Herbs*, by R. M. Bacon, p. 100. Yankee, 1972). Combine the lye and water. Melt the shortening. Add the olive oil to the shortening first, then the peanut oil. Now add the scent and stir. When both the lye and the oils reach 90° F., combine them and stir until thick. Pour into molds.

Molds for soap bars can be

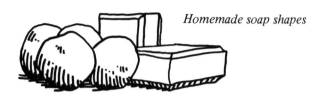

Homemade soap shapes

cardboard or wooden boxes, or you can work your soap into round balls before it has completely hardened. If you are searching for other shapes for your finished "best" soap, try a variety of plastic molds such as styrofoam egg cartons, plastic cookie cutters or trays, or make your own disposable plaster of Paris molds. Be sure to rub plaster or plastic molds with mineral oil to facilitate getting the soap out, or tear off the mold to expose the finished product.

If you settle for rectangular bars of homemade soap, you can bevel the edges or carve designs on their surfaces after removing them to "pretty them up." Save all the shavings for making soft soap for the bath.

In earlier times color was obtained by using vegetable dyes like beets, spinach and carrots. Blueberries and grapes were also commonly used. Today you can buy small vials of food coloring. Experiment by adding the coloring just before the soap is turned into the mold. (Wavy strips of color can be effected by stirring less or in different directions.)

Adding scent to soap is the real challenge. Natural herbal scents— lavender, rosemary, lemon balm— can be had by steeping plants in boiling water and substituting this amount of liquid in the amount called for in the recipe. (See: *The Forgotten Art of Growing, Gardening and Cooking with Herbs,* by R. M. Bacon, p. 102. Yankee, 1972.)

Essential oils can be purchased from some pharmacies, health food stores, hobby shops, herb shops and perfumery suppliers. These are concentrated fragrances. Candle scents (bought in wafer form) can also be used; dissolve the wafer in the lye.

Some of the most popular scents for special soaps are lavender, lemon, rosemary, rose, jasmine and carnation. Try one of these or make a bouquet using portions of several.

Once you have experience, it will be rewarding to experiment.

Reference
Bramson, A. S., *Soap: Making It, Using It, Enjoying It,* Workman Publishing Co., New York, 1972.

Yankee, Inc., Dublin, New Hampshire 03444

RICHARD M. BACON

The author and his family live as self-reliantly as possible on their small New Hampshire farm. Formerly a newspaper reporter and actor, he spent most of his professional life teaching at Collegiate School in New York City and Germantown Friends School in Philadelphia before a consuming passion for herbs and country living encouraged him to take up permanent residence and turn to farming and writing. A graduate of Williams College, he also studied in England at The London Academy of Music and Dramatic Art. He is the author of *The Forgotten Art of Growing, Gardening and Cooking with Herbs* and editor of *The Forgotten Art of Building a Stone Wall,* both published by Yankee, Inc., and has contributed articles to *Yankee, The Old Farmer's Almanac,* and *New Hampshire Profiles,* among other publications. Today, he and his family raise and process flowers for dried bouquets and sell herbs and herb products in the time left from tending a flock of sheep, geese, chickens, guinea hens, an all-purpose horse named Nellie Melba, and Maude, the family cow.